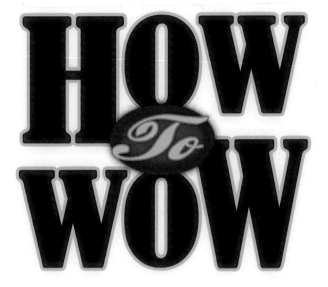

PHOTOSHOP CS3 FOR PHOTOGRAPHY

Jack Davis

Peachpit Press

How to Wow: Photoshop CS3 for Photography
Jack Davis

Peachpit Press
1249 Eighth Street
Berkeley, CA 94710
(510) 524-2178
(510) 524-2221 (fax)
Find us on the Web at:
www.peachpit.com
Peachpit Press is a division of Pearson Education.

ISBN 13: 978-0-321-50986-4
ISBN 10:   0-321-50986-2

9 8 7 6 5 4 3 2 1

Printed and bound in the United States of America

To *He* from whom all creative blessings flow!

And speaking of creative blessings, to our kids Ryan & Rachel— the smiling, passionate, and playful face of God that I get to see every single day!

Acknowledgments

First I want to thank Brie Gyncild, the incredibly talented freelance writer who threw herself into the very deep end of this often-painful project. Brie took the How to Wow instructional movies that I created with Software-Cinema and paraphrased them into the rough text that became this *Reader's Digest* edition of my dramatically more verbose disc and online training.

Brie even tackled rough layouts and wrote copy to fit, thus giving Jill (the world's greatest publication designer, my beautiful wife and resident partner-in-crime) starting pages to work with. Thank You Brie! And Thank You Jill!

And when in the ninth inning we needed another expert pair of eyes for one last round of edits, my coauthor from the *Photoshop Wow! Books* (and going way back to the *Verbum Magazine* days, for those of you who started with MacPaint), Linnea Dayton, stepped up to the plate and helped us hit another home run (knock on wood)! Thank you Linnea.

For years I've relied on many people for their support and constructive encouragement to help me become a better teacher, writer, artist, and human being. A mentor in this area for many years now has been renowned photographer and motivational speaker, Dewitt Jones. A more deliriously giddy and adventuresome cheerleader one could never find!

To the team at Software Cinema (www.software-cinema.com), thanks for working with me to try to create the best instructional resources possible.

I'd also like to thank renowned wedding photographer Brooke Christl (brookechristl.com), architectural photographer Mark Borosch (markborosch.com), and Lesa Snider King from iStockphoto.com for letting me use their exceptional photographs, and the many friends and associates who have put up with my incessant shooting of them for use as "stock"—specifically Gabby, Collene, Rachel, Nadine, Kevin, Devin, Dwanna, Dennis, Rylee, and the entire NCCC staff!

Also, we all owe much gratitude to the whole programming and marketing teams at Adobe for giving us the most phenomenally creative tool since the pencil, especially Julieanne Kost and Russell Brown, my fellow psychopathic speakers-in-arms.

Finally, thank you Peachpit Press and Nancy Ruenzel for catching the vision of the *How to Wow* series; it's been 15 years since we first embarked on a book together, and you haven't missed a beat! Thanks also to our editor Rebecca Gulick for putting up with the never-ending delays and the anal-retentive nature of us creative typos) and for helping us dot our i's and cross our t's, thank you to production manager David Van Ness, proofreader Liz Welch, and indexer Rebecca Plunkett.

—*Jack Davis*

Contents

I

WORKFLOW & OPTIMIZING
16

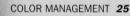

II

RETOUCHING & REPAIRING 82

III

ENHANCING & EMBELLISHING
154

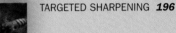

WELCOME TO CS3
Why write (or buy, for that matter) another book on Photoshop?

ART, IN ALL ITS FORMS—expressive, journalistic, didactic, commercial—matters! Creating beautiful visuals that speak to the heart is essential. Conveying the human condition, or the wonders of Creation, matters.

With Photoshop we have at our fingertips a tool of incredible power and grace to shape that art. *And with great power comes great... opportunity* (gotcha!), especially if you know **how** to create that **wow** experience that you want your audience to share.

This book's goal is to give you techniques, tips, insights, and essential principles that will help you achieve the highest **quality** results, with the greatest degree of "change-it-at-the-last moment" **flexibility**, utilizing practical yet elegant **speed**. This speed equates to the fewest number of steps necessary to complete what previously may have been an arduous Photoshop task, and it will actually allow you "extra" time to try creative variations, or maybe even to go home while the sun is still up (what a concept)!

So, why another book about Photoshop? The goal of maximizing the Quality, Flexibility, and Speed (and even Creative possibilities) of your work is constantly more accessible with each

incredible new version of our favorite digital darkroom. And the relatively small investment of time needed to truly digest the capabilities of each upgrade—especially the huge benefits that came with CS3's Camera Raw and Smart technologies—far outweighs the time lost to working "the way we've always done it."

I am *passionate* about the creative process and the art that is generated from that process; hopefully this book will help you strive to attain higher quality with your imagery, learn how make your files more flexible to allow for the request for last-minute changes that inevitably arise, and to apply speedier methodology so you can reach your artistic goals in a timely, more streamlined fashion.

By the way, the photographs used in the section and chapter spreads of the book are my own images (many taken on the road with a pocket camera), shared here purely to "cleanse the palate" from one chapter to the next (sometimes it's nice to share an image not for some principle or technique it illustrates, but simply because it floats your boat).

Here's to art!

New Features in Photoshop CS3

What's new in Photoshop CS3? Well, for starters, there are two versions now: Photoshop CS3 and Photoshop CS3 Extended. You can use this book with either version; they both include all the main image-editing features. Photoshop CS3 Extended adds some specific features intended for video, 3D, scientific image analysis, and other niches. Though many of the extended features are cool, they're not all that useful for photographers, so I don't cover them here.

See page 27 to learn how to locate this book's follow-along images, cinematic tutorials, downloadable freebies, and useful links!

- **Images on disc** so you can follow along with projects in this book
- **Software**—How to Wow ACR Presets and PhotoTools Lite!
- **Movies**—sample online instruction from Software Cinema
- **Discount codes** for indispensable third-party plug-ins and more!

Features for Photographers

These are the new Photoshop features you'll find most important as you edit images to tell your photographic story effectively and efficiently:

- **Bridge CS3:** Use Bridge to **organize, sort,** and **filter** your images; open them in Camera Raw or Photoshop; or even apply Camera Raw (ACR) settings directly.

- **Camera Raw 4:** Now you can use Camera Raw to edit **JPEG** and **TIFF** images as well as multiple raw formats. Camera Raw 4 provides greater precision and control, in addition to accelerated performance. You may never need to perform **global edits** in Photoshop again! As a matter of fact, one of my goals is to inspire you to shift over to working in Adobe Camera Raw (ACR) as much as possible.

- **Smart Filters:** Now you can apply filters that remain **live** and **editable**, and have their own layer mask. Any filter applied to a Smart Object is a nondestructive Smart Filter.

- **Quick Selection tool:** The Quick Selection tool analyzes the area you paint and **completes the selection** automatically. If the analysis isn't spot on, you can easily expand or contract the selection using Auto Align and Auto Blend (see below).

- **Refine Edge dialog box:** Use the Refine Edge dialog box to modify the edge of a **selection** before you begin editing. You can precisely **smooth, feather, contract,** or **expand** the current selection (**or mask**).

- **Auto Align** and **Auto Blend:** Automatically analyze content on multiple layers, and **move, distort** and **rotate** layers so they overlap as precisely as possible, then automatically **blend color** and **shading** into a merged image seamlessly. This technology is behind the Photomerge feature, and is especially useful when you create **panoramas.**

- **Black & White adjustment layer:** A one-button analysis of an image generates suggested conversion settings for simpler, faster, advanced black-and-white conversion. You can fine-tune the conversion with sliders and interactive eyedroppers.

- **Vanishing Point improvements:** Now you can use Vanishing Point to create **multiple planes** in any image, connected at any angle, for both adding to and removing parts of an image.

- **Redesigned Print dialog box: Preview** your image just before you print, reflecting your **color management** profiles. Controls are in one place to streamline printing. ▦

Optimizing the Photoshop CS3 Workspace

You'll save time and minimize frustration if you customize the Photoshop workspace to serve your specific needs. My recommendations are geared toward a streamlined workflow with a photography focus. You can create additional custom workspaces for other workflows, or modify this one to suit your needs.

Remove Unnecessary Icons

In the new interface, you can keep palettes handy as small icons, which take up a tiny amount of screen real estate. However, in my opinion, it's more of a distraction than a shortcut. Therefore, it's a good idea to **remove** icons for palettes you don't need to use on a regular basis. To delete an icon, first click it to open its palette, and then click the "x" in the palette tab **A**.

The default workspace has an extra column of icons to the left of the main docked palettes **B**. I immediately remove the Tool Presets, Brushes, Character, and Paragraph icons, because each of those features are easily accessible in the **Options bar.** I also delete the Layer Comps icon because I don't use that palette often, unless I'm creating variations for a graphic design project.

Rearrange Palettes

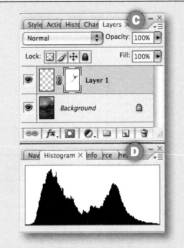

To organize palettes in Photoshop CS3, you **dock** them and then expand or contract them as needed. The dock is permanently attached to the top of the document window. If you want a palette to **float** freely, drag its tab out of the dock.

You may **customize** the palettes to suit the way you work. Drag a palette's tab to move it to a new position in its palette group. To change the stacking order of palette groups in the dock, click the title bar for the palette group **C**, and then drag it into place above or below another group **D**. Look for the **blue line** to know when the palette or group is over the correct spot to let go. You can also resize palette groups by dragging the lower-right corner.

The palettes I use frequently fit into a single stack in the dock. The top palette group fills most of the dock. It contains the palettes that display lists Layers, Channels, Actions, History, and Styles. In the bottom palette group, much shorter than the top, are the Info, Histogram, Navigator, Swatches, and Clone Source palettes. I close the Color and Paths palettes, as I rarely use them.

Customize Menus

New...	⌘N
Open...	⌘O
Browse...	⌥⌘O
Open As Smart Object...	
Open Recent	▶
Device Central...	
Close	⌘W
Close All	⌥⌘W
Close and Go To Bridge...	⇧⌘W
Save	⌘S
Save As...	⇧⌘S

You can also customize the menus in Photoshop CS3 to remove items you don't need, and to highlight items with specific colors.

To customize the menus, choose Edit > Menus. In the Keyboard Shortcuts and Menus dialog box, choose a set of menus from the Set menu. Choose whether you want to change application menus or palette menus. Expand the name of the menu you want to change.

- To hide an item, click its Visibility button.

- To show an item that was previously hidden, click the empty Visibility button.

- To add color to an item, click the color swatch (or the word None, if no color has been applied), and choose a color.

- To save the custom menu set, click the Save Set As icon. Then name the new menu set, and click Save.

TIP

CS3 Changes Made Clear. Photoshop CS3 comes with several preconfigured *workspaces*. The one called What's New – CS3 highlights every menu item that has changed from previous versions. It's a great way to see what's new.

Save Custom Workspace

As in previous versions of Photoshop, you can save your custom workspace. In fact, you may want to save multiple workspaces for different tasks, such as retouching or repairing images, color correction, or working with panoramas. It's much faster to apply a customized workspace than it is to open and close or rearrange palettes each time.

To save a workspace you've customized, click Workspace on the right side of the Options bar. Choose Save Workspace, name the workspace, and then select which of the workspace components you want to include. You can save the palette locations, customized keyboard shortcuts, and menus.

To apply a workspace, click Workspace, and then choose the name of the workspace you want to apply.

INSIGHT

Tab Out, Hover In. To quickly hide all the palettes, press the Tab key; to hide only the Tools palette, press Shift+Tab. (Press Shift+Tab again, and the Tools palette is visible but the others are hidden.) When the palettes are hidden, you can display them temporarily by moving your cursor over the right or left side of the screen. That way, they take up screen space only when you need them.

Set Photoshop Preferences

Several options in the **Preferences** dialog box can make your life easier. To open it, choose Edit > Preferences (Windows) or Photoshop > Preferences (Mac OS) and choose General.

In the **General** pane, turn off **Export Clipboard.** This option converts and saves the clipboard content every time you leave Photoshop, thereby slowing down the switch from application to application.

Choose **Bicubic Sharper** from the **Image Interpolation** menu. Bicubic Sharper gives the best results for batch processing the scale-down of images. If you need to enlarge an image, use the Image Size dialog box, and change the setting there to Bicubic Smoother.

In the **File Handling** pane, select **Prefer Adobe Camera Raw For JPEG Files** so you can use Camera Raw (ACR) when you open JPEG files within Photoshop.

If you want to use plug-ins from older versions of Photoshop, enter your older Photoshop serial number in the Plug-ins pane, and locate the folder that has the older plug-ins. If you have a Mac with an Intel processor, update your plug-ins to take advantage of your processor speed.

In the **Type** pane, set the **Font Preview Size** to your preferred size. There's now a **Huge** option so you can make design decisions directly from the menu! ⌨

More Preferences for JPEGs

Making Adobe Camera Raw (ACR) the foundation of your workflow for all your images—JPEG, TIFF and Raw—is only possible in CS3 if you give all three programs (Bridge, ACR, and Photoshop) permission to play nicely with these various file formats. Here's how.

Bridge and Photoshop Preferences

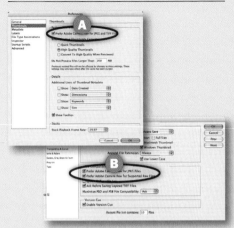

Start by setting the preferences in Bridge itself. Choose Edit > Preferences (Windows) or Bridge CS3 > Preferences (Mac OS) to open the Preferences dialog box.

In the Thumbnails pane, select **Prefer Adobe Camera Raw For JPEG And TIFF Files A**, so that you can make the same adjustments to JPEG and TIFF files that you can to raw files. While you're there, select High Quality Thumbnails so that thumbnails in the Content panel will reflect changes you make in Camera Raw (ACR).

In the Cache pane (Windows) or the Advanced pane (Mac OS), select Automatically Export Caches To Folders When Possible. With this option selected, changes you make in ACR will travel with the images when you move them.

In Photoshop, choose Edit > Preferences > File Handling (Windows) or Photoshop > Preferences > File Handling (Mac OS). Select **Prefer Adobe Camera Raw For JPEG Files** and **Prefer Adobe Camera Raw For Supported Raw Files B**. Now you'll have access to ACR even if you open an image within Photoshop rather than Bridge.

Camera Raw Preferences

Now, set things up in Camera Raw (ACR) and Photoshop for your smart workflow: In Bridge, choose Edit > Camera Raw Preferences (Windows) or Bridge CS3 > Camera Raw Preferences (Mac OS). Select **Always Open JPEG Files With Settings Using Camera Raw and Always Open TIFF Files With Settings Using Camera Raw C**. With this option selected, manipulations you make to an image in ACR will also show up in Photoshop.

Finally, in ACR, click the workflow options text link at the bottom **D**, and select **Open In Photoshop As Smart Objects** in the Workflow Options dialog box **E**. 🖩

TIP

Saving as an Image. Smart Objects are so useful that you'll want to open most of your images as Smart Objects in Photoshop. However, if you want to open a file as an image, press Shift to change the **Open Object** button to an **Open Image** button.

We must remember that a photograph can hold just as much as we put into it, and no one has ever approached the full possibilities of the medium.

—ANSEL ADAMS

WORKFLOW & OPTIMIZING

CHAPTER 1
Camera and Computer Workflow

©JHDAVIS

LET US ALL BE REMINDED: The most important tool in the photographic process is not Photoshop (gulp), but rather, the camera. A window to the world, the camera shapes the story, the moment you are attempting to capture. The lens, aperture, shutter speed, even ISO and file format all determine what you will have at your disposal when you're alone with Photoshop, the world's most remarkable digital darkroom.

To "develop" your images, you must have your essentials prepped and ready for use. In a traditional photo lab, chemicals, papers, and enlargers must be ready to go. In our case, the camera and computer must be configured before crafting a print in Photoshop can begin.

A Savvy Digital Camera Workflow

Any experienced cook knows that the secret to a successful meal is starting with high-quality ingredients. "Garbage in, garbage out" as the saying goes. The same is true in photography. Photoshop provides a vast range of very powerful tools, but to convey a story worth telling presupposes you took the time necessary to capture the best possible image in the beginning.

Digital cameras—even pocket-size models—come with many bells and whistles. Among those options are some key settings that can make a world of difference in your photos. Understanding these settings and knowing how to use them will save you time and frustration later.

1. Choose a Format

Digital cameras can capture photos in various flavors of three primary formats: Raw, JPEG, and TIFF.

If your camera offers a raw format, use it! *Raw* file formats give you the broadest reproducibility, and the flexibility to change much of your data nondestructively long after the photo is taken. Raw files don't even contain pixels; they hold the raw sensor data gathered when you pressed the shutter, as close as you'll get to the digital negative. Information such as white balance and color space, set in your camera, comes along with the file, but is not permanently embedded.

If a raw format isn't available, shoot in the highest-quality *JPEG* format available, with the least amount of compression. With a JPEG, camera settings become much more important, as they're "cooked into" the file and turned into colored pixels.

Some cameras let you shoot both raw and JPEG formats concurrently. If the JPEG looks perfect, you may not need the raw file, but having it available gives you tremendous flexibility.

2. Choose a Color Space

The color space determines the range of colors available, and how the color is mapped within the file. The same image can look very different when you apply different color spaces. When you shoot raw images, you can change the color space of the image later, but when you shoot JPEG images, the camera's color space becomes very important.

If your camera supports it, use the **Adobe RGB** color space. It was designed for photography, with a broad color gamut (the reproducible range of colors). It's your best choice for images you'll be tweaking in Photoshop, or for printing.

sRGB is the default color space in most digital cameras, and it's the Windows default color space. It's a great color space for business graphics and for the Web, but it wasn't designed for photography. Though you may need to save images with the sRGB color space for use on the Web later, Adobe RGB gives you more flexibility while you're editing photos.

Even if you shoot in a raw file format, set the color space to Adobe RGB so that you'll view images accurately on the camera. The image you see on the back of your camera is determined by the camera's settings, even though they're not permanently embedded in the raw file. If your camera supports only an sRGB color space, don't lose sleep over it, that'll do.

3. Choose an ISO Setting

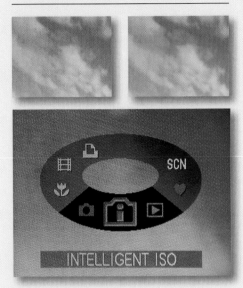

The ISO setting determines how sensitive the camera's sensors are to light, just as the film speed in traditional photography indicates the film's sensitivity to light. Increased sensitivity usually means more noise will be apparent in the image. Therefore, you'll want to keep your ISO setting as low as possible for the current lighting.

Many cameras offer an **Auto ISO** feature, which lets your camera adjust the ISO setting as needed. You may even be able to set the maximum sensitivity, so the Auto ISO can only raise the sensitivity so high.

Additionally, some cameras have a feature called **Intelligent ISO,** which takes into consideration the brightness of the scene *and* camera shake to set the ISO appropriately.

> **T I P**
>
> **ExpoDisc.** An ExpoDisc, or ExpoCap, fits over your lens so you can easily take an accurate custom white balance setting. **For info, visit expodisc.com.**

4. Set the White Balance

The white balance setting determines what the camera identifies as white, and the relationship of all other colors. When the white balance is appropriate for your lighting, colors in the image are rendered accurately. However, when the white balance is off, the image may appear warm (yellow-red) or cool (blue-green).

You can easily adjust the white balance in raw images long after the shot, and still achieve perfect quality. When you shoot JPEG images, however, the white balance setting in the camera is crucial. If you're shooting under artificial light, choose the appropriate light type (candescent, incandescent, etc.) in the camera, or you may get better results creating a custom white balance.

You can use an **ExpoDisc A** or simply point at a white wall to take a **custom white balance** setting before you even take the shot. If you want to adjust the white balance later, include a reference color in the scene—using a professional reference card from Gretag Macbeth **B** or WhiBal **C**, or in a pinch, a gray lens cleaning cloth—that will provide a clear reference point in Photoshop or Camera Raw to neutralize a color cast.

5. Set Other Camera Options

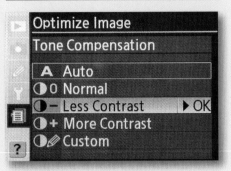

In some cases, turning camera options off or down may improve your images. Consider turning off **noise reduction**, or turn it down as low as possible, because you can often perform the same task more successfully in ACR and even third-party software, such as Imagenomics' Noiseware Pro (see adventuresinphotoshop.com). The exception is a feature called **Long Exposure Noise Reduction**, which is quite effective when you're shooting on a tripod in a dark setting, for instance photographing stars or a cityscape at night.

For raw images, turn **tone compensation** (or whatever your camera calls it) down to lower the contrast. Your images won't have as much pop on the back of the camera, but the review on the back of the camera will be more accurate. For both Raw and JPEG images, turning down tone compensation gives you more detail in the highlights and shadows—important if you're editing in Photoshop. Remember that the more intense the contrast and saturation in your original image, the less latitude you'll have in Photoshop. (If you're shooting JPEG images that you won't be editing in Photoshop, DON'T reduce the contrast setting.)

You may also want to reduce **image sharpening**, if your camera offers it, because you can typically sharpen images more effectively in either Photoshop or Camera Raw.

6. Take the Photo

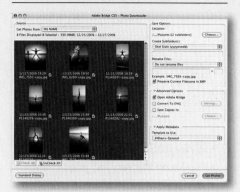

In most cases, you'll get the most information in your images if you expose your image brighter, rather than darker, so long as the resulting image doesn't have **clipping** (loss of important detail) in the highlights. If you're used to overexposing when you shoot with negative film, you'll want to develop new habits. Digital cameras won't capture highlight information in overexposed images—and you will lose shadow detail with underexposure. However, if you have to weight the image one direction, lean toward lighter exposure. There's always more data in the highlights than the shadows, providing greater control in Camera Raw and Photoshop to get the best possible shadow and highlight detail.

Remember to adjust the aperture! The **aperture**, measured as f/stop, is the opening in your camera; it sets the depth-of-field, which determines how much of your image is in focus. The smaller the aperture, the larger the depth-of-field (and the larger the f/stop number). For landscapes, use a larger setting so that everything is in focus; for portraits, use a smaller setting (such as 5.6) to blur the background.

> ### INSIGHT
>
> **Setting Priorities.** In many digital cameras, you can set the priority for how an exposure is made. Typically, you'll have the best results if you prioritize aperture so you can control how much of your photo is in focus.

7. Transfer and Catalog

Of course, to make adjustments to your images, you must first transfer them from the camera to a hard drive. Connect the camera to the computer using the cable that came with it, or insert the camera's card directly into a card reader.

Bridge CS3 includes a utility called **Photo Downloader (File > Get Photos from Camera)**. When you connect your camera or card to the computer, Photo Downloader can automatically transfer images, name them according to your instructions, apply the appropriate metadata, place them into subfolders, and open them in Bridge. It will even automatically convert the images into Adobe's DNG format for you.

Once the images are on your hard drive, you can sort, organize, stack, and rank them in Bridge. You can apply metadata templates and add keywords as well.

> ### TIP
>
> **Handling CDs and DVDs.** CDs and DVDs may look resilient, but their surfaces are actually quite fragile. Handle them by the edges, use only acid-free markers on the label side, and store them out of the light. Perhaps counterintuitively, the side closest to the data is the label side, so be especially careful not to scratch it.

8. Archive Images

As you work with an image, you'll save it in different formats for different purposes. It's a good idea to save the **original** image in a raw, JPEG, or DNG format so that you can always return to it. In fact, you should also archive these files to a CD, DVD, or removable hard drive so that they're safe in the event of hard drive failure.

Later, when you're working on files in Photoshop, save them in the native PSD file format so that you continue to have access to all the layers, Smart Objects, Smart Filters, and other Photoshop attributes. Save a layered PSD file as your **master file,** which you can continue to return to when you need to modify and adapt it for future projects.

Finally, when you've prepared the file for use in a specific context, such as a Web site or printed page, you may **save a copy** in PSD, TIFF or JPEG format. You can scale this version for specific printing purposes, convert color for specific profiles, or make other changes, without affecting your master PSD file. ▥

Finding the Optimal Exposure

Use your camera's Histogram feature to determine if you are getting the best exposure for a scene. The histogram shows you where you may be losing detail in your image, both in the shadows and in the highlights. You'll learn more about histograms in Chapter 5, "Color and Tone Optimizing," but you can start taking advantage of the histogram in your camera right away.

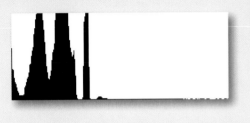

Underexposure

A tall spike on the very left edge of the histogram indicates that an area of the image is solid black. That usually means you've underexposed the image, losing shadow detail in the process. If you need that shadow detail for the scene you are trying to capture, move the exposure compensation setting on your camera to a positive number so that it will use more light, and then shoot the image again. If you have trouble finding an exposure that eliminates the spike on the left without creating one on the right, refer to the bottom of this page for help with tricky exposures.

Overexposure

A tall spike on the very right edge of the histogram indicates that an area of the image is pure white. That spike usually means you've overexposed the image, losing highlight detail. To capture the highlight detail, move the exposure compensation setting on your camera to a negative number so that it will use less light, and then shoot the photo again. If you know you'll be adjusting your image in Photoshop, remember you'll usually get better results when you darken lighter images than when you lighten darker images, which typically reveals artifacts such as noise.

Tricky Exposures

Sometimes no exposure compensation setting on your camera can strike the perfect balance for a scene: you'd sacrifice either shadow detail or highlight detail. In those cases, you may be better off taking two or more exposures—one overexposed **A** and one underexposed **B**—and combining them in Photoshop **C**. For multiple exposures, use a tripod to steady the shot, and keep the aperture consistent, so your depth-of-field won't change between shots. 🖩

> ### INSIGHT
>
> **Using the Bracketing Feature.** Some cameras will take multiple shots at different exposures for you. Look for a bracketing feature (possibly listed as BKT) in a pocket camera. When this feature is enabled, the camera usually takes three shots: one at what it interprets as good, or "metered," exposure, one shot underexposed, and one overexposed. You can then take the highlight and shadow detail from each of the images. ▶ **See page 78 for how to combine bracketed exposures.**

Calibration and Color Profiles

Color management systems are only as good as the data they're given. To ensure that your color profiles contain accurate information for the devices you use (including your monitor, printers, scanners, and so on), calibrate the devices and thus create the custom profiles that Photoshop will use to ensure that what you see is what you get.

Calibrating Your Monitor

Color management begins with your monitor. Before you do anything else, you need to calibrate your monitor to neutralize any color cast or tonal deviation. Then, create a custom color profile that describes the way the monitor displays colors, as well as its brightness. Most calibration tools will automatically create a custom profile for you—and they'll even pop it into the right folder for your system. If you're serious about color management, invest in a color calibration hardware (typically referred to as a "puck") or software package), to automate the process of correcting your monitor and creating the most accurate profiles. I live by the award-winning x-rite, i1DesignLT, which includes the i1Pro device and the i1Match software (pictured). If you don't have the hardware, you can get started using the Calibrate button in the Color panel of the Displays system preference in Mac OS X. Or for Windows, use Adobe Gamma, a utility that comes with Photoshop in Windows.

Creating Color Profiles for Printers and Papers

Printer manufacturers usually include color profiles on the printer's installation disc, and they may provide additional profiles for papers on a Web site. To obtain the most accurate results, you can create a custom profile for your printer and the specific paper stock you're using. You can visit a Web site such as chromix.com to arrange to send them a special print sample from a file they provide; they'll email you back a custom print profile. Or you can pay about $2,000 for a **spectrophotometer** to create your own custom profiles in-house.

Place custom profiles in the Library/Colorsync/Profiles folder in Mac OS X; in Windows, simply right-click the profile and choose Install Profile.

Using Scanner Profiles

If you're scanning images, a color profile can produce more accurate scans. A scanner profile is less important than monitor and printer profiles, however, because most scans will be color-corrected and adjusted in Photoshop. If you want to create a profile for your scanner, consider software applications such as Monaco EZColor. To use the application, scan the provided sample color swatches, then run the results through the software. ▥

Color Management

Ideally, the color you see on your monitor will match the color on your final printed page. The key to consistent color is color management, which relies on color profiles to describe the color information for each monitor, printer, scanner, and so on. With accurate color profiles and a little know-how, you can smoothly move images from one device to another.

What to Do When Profiles Are Missing

When you create a new document, Photoshop automatically assigns a profile based on the current working space options in the Color Settings dialog box. When you open an existing image (if your Color Settings are configured as recommended in the tip at the left), as a default Photoshop warns you if the image has no profile embedded, or if it differs from the working profile.

If the profile is missing, in most cases you'll want to select **Leave As Is,** and then assign a profile after you've finished opening the image. The dialog box that appears when you open an image has no Preview option (because the image hasn't opened yet), so if you assign a profile then, you're working blind. However, you're able to preview the results when you use the Assign Profile command after opening the image.

On the other hand, if you know you're going to assign a particular profile, go ahead and do it when the missing profile warning appears. If you are confident, save a few steps by having Photoshop automatically convert the profile to the working color space as well.

Assigning and Converting to Profiles

A big difference exists between *assigning profiles and converting to profiles.* When you *assign* a profile, the appearance of the image changes on the screen. When you *convert* to a profile, Photoshop maps the colors of the current profile to the colors in the new profile, so that you can use the image on a different device, but the colors on your monitor remain as close as possible to the original.

Assign profiles to images with no existing profile, such as screenshots. To assign a profile, choose Edit > Assign Profile, and then choose the profile you want to use. Select the Preview option in the Assign Profile dialog box to see the effect.

When preparing an image for a destination that requires a specific color profile, *convert* to that profile. For example, to use an image on the Web, you need to convert its profile from Adobe RGB to sRGB. Choose Edit > Convert To Profile, and choose the destination profile.

Soft-Proofing in Photoshop

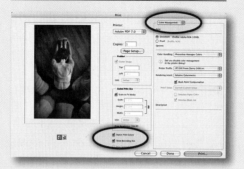

With a calibrated system and accurate color profiles, you can **soft-proof** your image directly on the monitor. Choose View > Proof Setup > Custom to create a custom proof condition. Select the profile for the device you want to simulate, and if possible, use a profile that is specific to the paper and ink type you'll be using. Printer profiles are typically installed with the printer; if you don't see the one you need, check the printer CD or the printer or paper manufacturer's Web site for additional profiles.

Once you've chosen the profile, choose View > Proof Colors (Command+Y or Ctrl+Y). The document remains unchanged, but the monitor approximates the appearance of the printed image.

▶ **To learn more about soft-proofing, see "Soft Proofing and Print Previewing" on page 200.**

Printing

When you're ready to print, choose File > Print. Select the **Match Print Colors** option in the Print dialog box to display an accurate color preview. Then, choose Color Management from the pop-up menu at the top of the dialog box. For Color Handling, choose Photoshop Manages Colors. Choose a Printer Profile for printer, paper, and ink. For example, you would select the profile SP2200 Premium Glossy_PK for printing to the Epson 2200 on their Premium Glossy paper, using their Photo Black ink set. Choose Relative Colorimetric for the Rendering Intent, and select Black Point Compensation. (These settings work well for most images, if you have an accurate printer profile. However, some people prefer the Perceptual rendering intent. Experiment to see what works best for your images.)

When you click Print, Photoshop opens the dialog box for your specific printer. There, turn off the printer's color management, so that it doesn't interfere with Photoshop color management, but remember to set the paper setting to match the paper you'll be printing on.

▶ **See Chapter 15 beginning on page 190 for more on proofing and printing.**

Converting Images to CMYK

Much of your work in Photoshop will be done in an RGB color space, but commercial printers often require images delivered in the CMYK color space. To convert a flattened copy of your image **(never convert your master layered PSD file to CMYK; always work on a copy)**, first choose Edit > Color Settings, and select the appropriate profile from the Working Spaces CMYK pop-up menu. (If your printing company gave you settings, select Custom CMYK, and adjust the settings in the dialog box that appears.) Close the Color Settings dialog, and choose Image > Mode > CMYK Color.

To soft-proof your RGB file **before** converting to CMYK, choose View > Proof Setup > Working CMYK. Then choose View > Proof Colors. ▥

Don't Forget the *How to Wow Follow-Along Images* and Free Downloadable Goodies!

Companion CD-ROM

The majority of the images used in the step-by-step projects in *How to Wow: Photoshop CS3 for Photography* can be found on the companion CD located in the back of this book. (Unfortunately not all the images are available due to copyright restrictions.) These files are organized into folders based on the chapter in which they occur.

Companion Web Site

ADVENTURESINPHOTOSHOP.COM

Our Web page **AdventuresInPhotoshop.com** contains a plethora of links to some truly great stuff that I encourage you to use, as they will enhance your **How to Wow** learning experience.

POWERFUL PRESETS

First you'll find a special link to **OnOne Software,** and the installer they have created for my *How to Wow PhotoPresets for Adobe Camera Raw* (and my *How to Wow PhotoPresets for Lightroom* as well). These presets and how they can fit into your workflow are discussed starting on page 43. You'll also find video tutorials on the basics of using these presets.

INCREDIBLE SOFTWARE

Just as useful, but with even greater sex appeal, is a special *Lite* version of the software I created with OnOne: **PhotoTools Lite.** This truncated but completely functional version of PhotoTools gives you access to 20 of my very best photo enhancement techniques that you can mix, match, save as your own, and batch process to your heart's content!

LIGHTS, CAMERA, ONLINE MOVIES

Next you'll find links for free How to Wow movies, including some of my favorite techniques from this book, that are part of **Software Cinema's** online **Workshops on Demand.**

TIMESAVING SCRIPTS

Something not to miss is a link to the Tips & Techniques section of the **Russell Brown Show,** where you can download **Dr. Brown's Services.** Used repeatedly in this book, Dr. Brown's Services is an indispensable set of custom Photoshop Scripts that I use regularly. Here you will also find some funky but extremely useful tutorials on all things Photoshop.

DISCOUNTS FOR THIRD-PARTY TOOLS

In addition to the free downloadable goodies, there are links (and codes for substantial discounts) to some Third Party Photoshop Plug-ins that I find absolutely life-saving, such as Imagenomic's **Noiseware Pro,** Nik Software's **Viveza,** and OnOne's **PhotoFrame Pro.**

FOR THE FUN OF IT

Last but not least, you'll find links to some downright fun stuff, such as an article from *Outdoor Photographer* writer Dewitt Jones and myself about the creative power of point-n-click cameras (with links and samples, including information on infrared camera conversions).

CAUTION

Copyright Heads-up. Please note, these copyrighted images are to be used for education purposes only. Download them in order to work along with the tutorials in the book, but please do not use them for any other purpose—personal or commercial— and do not share them in any way with anyone else (you're special!). Thanks!

CHAPTER 2
Bridge and Camera Raw Workflow

NOT SINCE THE INTRODUCTION of Layers in Photoshop 3 has there been the potential for such a significant change in the creative workflow, on account of the incredible and supremely practical enhancements to Adobe Camera Raw (also referred to as ACR) and the spectacular Smart Filter technology (covered in the next chapter).

These significantly improved technologies, in concert with Bridge's plethora of organization and automation tools, finally allow the user to stop endlessly pushing pixels and focus instead on the process of creating the most powerful photographic imagery possible!

Bridge CS3 Essentials

Think of Bridge as home base for your images. You can use Bridge CS3 to download images from your camera, add metadata, compare photographs to each other, and organize all your images. Customize the workspace to give yourself easy access to the features you use most often, and to increase the size of the preview so you can easily see what you're working with.

Importing Images

The Photo Downloader utility imports images directly into Bridge from your camera or memory card. Connect your camera to your computer or insert a card. Then, choose File > Get Photos From Camera. The Photo Downloader dialog box displays thumbnails of all the images on the camera or card **A**. (Click Advanced Dialog if you don't see them **B**.) Deselect any images you don't want to import. Click Choose to select a location for the imported images **C**. You can also rename the files so that they're easier for you to recognize, but the original filename is still preserved in the metadata (XMP).

Additionally, you can choose to have Bridge open automatically when you import images, and to convert images to DNG format, save a copy of the images to a second location, and apply metadata, such as your name and a basic copyright notice **D**.

Click Get Photos to import the images.

Adding Metadata

Metadata is information about an image, such as the date it was shot, camera settings, and keywords. Metadata makes it easier to filter and organize your images.

The easiest way to apply metadata is with a **metadata template** that includes your contact information, copyright information, and any keywords you want to add to all the images. You can apply the metadata template in the Photo Downloader dialog box. Or select images in Bridge and choose Tools > Append Metadata to apply it.

Though you can use the Tools > Create Metadata Template command to customize a template, I prefer to use the File Info fields. Choose File > File Info, customize the template, and choose Save Metadata Template from the pop-up menu in the upper-right corner.

Comparing Images

©JHDAVIS

To view two or more images side-by-side, select them in the Content panel. (Shift-click to select images that are next to each other; Ctrl-click in Windows or Command-click in Mac OS if they're not.) Bridge displays up to nine selected images in the Preview panel.

The new **Loupe tool** lets you magnify portions of an image, so that you can check focus or otherwise analyze an image or compare it with another. To use the Loupe tool, move the cursor over the image in the Preview panel. By default, it magnifies to 100%. To zoom in further, press the plus (+) key; to zoom out, press the minus (–) key. To close the Loupe tool, just click within the magnified area.

You can move the Loupe tool around within an image, and you can display Loupe tools for multiple images in the Preview panel; simply click each image. To synchronize movement of Loupe tools in multiple images, press the Command/Ctrl key as you drag the magnified area.

Stacking Images

If you were working with traditional slides on a light table, you'd probably stack them according to subject matter or other criteria off to the side when you weren't working with them. In Bridge CS3, you can also stack images. Stacking images helps keep the Content panel free of clutter, without removing any of your images.

To stack images, select them, then choose Stacks > Group As Stack (or click Command/Ctrl-G). The stack appears as a single thumbnail in the Content panel; a number indicates how many images are in the stack.

To see all the images in a stack, select it and choose Stacks > Open Stack, or just click the number. The image thumbnails appear separately in the Content panel, but a border indicates that they are still part of the stack. To collapse, or close, the stack again, click the number. When I press Command/Ctrl-left arrow key, it closes the whole folder. Shift-click the back edge of the stack to toggle between displaying all images in the Preview panel and just the top image.

Stacks make it easy to add keywords or apply metadata to multiple images at once. You can also use a stack to create a panorama using the Photomerge feature from Photoshop (in Bridge choose Tools > Photoshop > Photomerge).

If you no longer want images to be stacked, select the stack and then choose Stacks > Ungroup From Stack.

Labeling Images

Identifying your images is easy using star ratings or colored labels. I use the colored labels to organize images by subject. You can also use them to note the quality of images, what they require, or anything else you like. To apply a colored label, select the image(s), choose Label, and select a color or a label name. To rename the labels associated with each label, choose Edit > Preferences (Windows) or Bridge CS3 > Preferences (Mac OS), select Labels from the list, and then type new labels.

To apply a star rating, select the image, choose Label, and choose a star rating. (You can simply use the left and right arrow keys to cycle through images, and tap the keyboard shortcut to apply the star rating or a colored label).

Sorting Images

The new Filter panel is a huge timesaver. It lets you quickly sort through images, displaying only the ones with specific metadata, star ratings, or colored labels. For example, to see only the images with the keyword Aspen, select Aspen. To see only images with the keyword Aspen that were shot on a particular date, select the keyword *and* the date. You can quickly drill down to the images you want.

You're not limited to the images in a single folder, either. Click the icon of the file folder just below the Filter tab to view the contents of the selected folder and all of its subfolders; click the icon again to see only a single folder's contents. (In the previous version of Bridge, you had to use the Find File command to find images in subfolders.)

INSIGHT

Rejection Isn't So Bad. Bridge CS3 gives an image a second chance when you decide not to keep it. When you click the Delete icon, Bridge asks whether you want to reject the files or delete them. If you reject them, a Reject label is applied to the images—another handy way to filter images you may want to reconsider later.

Customizing the Workspace

Bridge CS3 comes with some preset workspaces, but I prefer to create my own, and encourage you to do so as well.

To move a panel, drag its tab into a new position. Move the **Preview panel** to the middle of the workspace, so that there is more room to view the image and so you can see both horizontal and vertical images without a major shift in the apparent size of the images. Move the Content panel to the right side, keeping the Metadata, Keywords, and Content panels on the right side of the window, and the Favorites, Folders, and Filter panels on the left.

To save a custom workspace, choose Window > Workspace > Save Workspace, name it, and click Save.

To use the workspace, choose Window > Workspace and then choose the workspace you saved. Numbered icons in the bottom-right corner give quick access to workspaces. To assign a workspace to an icon, click the arrow next to it, and then choose the workspace.

TIP

Purge the Cache. If Bridge is sluggish, try purging the cache. If you've exported the cache to a folder, you have nothing to lose. Click Purge Cache in the Cache pane (Windows) or the Advanced pane (Mac OS) of the Preferences dialog box.

Setting Preferences

You'll work more efficiently in Bridge if you adjust a few of the preferences.

Choose Edit > Preferences (Windows) or Bridge CS3 > Preferences (Mac OS) to open the Preferences dialog box.

In the General pane, select **Double-Click Edits Camera Raw Settings In Bridge** so you can edit images in Camera Raw without also opening Photoshop.

In the Thumbnails pane, select **High Quality Thumbnails** to ensure that you're seeing accurate previews of images you've edited in Camera Raw. Then, select **Prefer Camera Raw For JPEG And TIFF Files** to open JPEG and TIFF images in Camera Raw.

In the Cache pane (Windows) or the Advanced pane (Mac OS), select **Automatically Export Caches To Folders When Possible.** The caches contain the high-resolution preview and thumbnails; exporting them sends those thumbnails with your images when you back them up. ▥

Batch Processing Made Easy

Go beyond the Batch Process feature that comes with Bridge. Dr. Brown's 1-2-3 Process gives greater control and better results with minimal effort.

RUSSELL BROWN

HTW See page 27 to learn how to locate this book's follow-along images, cinematic tutorials, downloadable freebies, and useful links!

1. Download Dr. Brown's Services

Russell Brown, one of Adobe's resident mad scientists, and his team have cooked up some terrific custom scripts for Photoshop. The best news is that they're free! Go to www.adventuresinphotoshop.com (where most of the links mentioned in this book are located), click on the caricature of Russell, and scroll down to look for Dr. Brown's Services Easy Installer for Mac OS or Windows.

Download and install the scripts, which become accessible in Bridge or Photoshop. Restart Bridge after you install the scripts.

2. Open Dr. Brown's 1-2-3 Process

In Bridge, select the images you want to modify. Then choose Tools > Dr. Brown's Services > Dr. Brown's 1-2-3 Process.

Dr. Brown's 1-2-3 Process

1. Select the images to process
   Process files from Bridge only (4)

   [Run]
   [Cancel]

2. Select location to save processed images
   ⦿ Save in Same Location ☑ Save in sub-folder
   ○ [Select Folder...] No folder has been selected

   [Load...]
   [Save...]

3. File Types

   ① ☑ Save as: [PSD ⬍] Set sub-folder name: [Set 1]   ☐ Resize to Fit
      ☑ Maximize Compatibility ☑ Flatten Images   W: [   ] [pixels ⬍]
      Output Profile: [Same as Source ⬍]   H: [   ] [pixels ⬍]
      ☑ Run Action: [After Image Resize ⬍]   Resolution: [72] [pixels/inch ⬍]
      Select Action: [Default Actions ⬍] [Sepia Toning (layer) ⬍]   [Bicubic ⬍]

   ② ☑ Save as: [TIFF ⬍] Set sub-folder name: [Set 2]   ☐ Resize to Fit
      ☑ LZW Compression ☑ Flatten Images   W: [   ] [pixels ⬍]
      Output Profile: [Working CMYK ⬍]   H: [   ] [pixels ⬍]
      ☐ Run Action: [After Image Resize ⬍]   Resolution: [72] [pixels/inch ⬍]
      Select Action: [Default Actions ⬍] [Vignette (selection) ⬍]   [Bicubic ⬍]

   ③ ☑ Save as: [JPEG ⬍] Set sub-folder name: [Set 3]   ☑ Resize to Fit
      Quality: [7] ☑ Remove preview and metadata for reduced file size   W: [500] [pixels ⬍]
      Output Profile: [sRGB IEC61966-2.1 ⬍]   H: [500] [pixels ⬍]
      ☐ Run Action: [After Image Resize ⬍]   Resolution: [72] [pixels/inch ⬍]
      Select Action: [Default Actions ⬍] [Vignette (selection) ⬍]   [Bicubic Sharper ⬍]

4. Preferences

3. Select Options

In the Dr. Brown's 1-2-3 Process dialog box, specify a location for the final files after Photoshop has finished processing them.

You may run three different batch processes at one time. In each case, select the format for the final file, the file quality or compression, and the output color profile. If you want to run an action, choose one from the menu. You can specify other settings, such as the interpolation method, if you resize the image. (Choose Bicubic Sharper if you're reducing the image size!) If you're saving a file for the Web, you may remove the preview and metadata to reduce the file size.

Be sure to select the option to tag files with copyright information, especially if you're removing the metadata.

If you expect to run these processes again, save the settings. Click Save to save the settings, and give them a name you'll recognize. Later, to use the settings, click Load and locate the preset you saved.

INSIGHT

Batch Rename. If you simply need to rename files, select them in Bridge, and then choose Tools > Batch Rename. Add text, sequence numbers, extensions, metadata—anything you want to include in the filename. You may also preserve the original filename in the XMP metadata so you can search on it later.

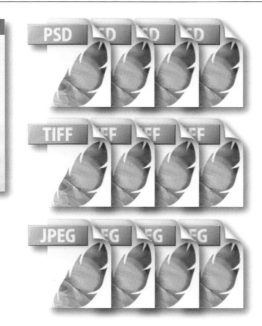

4. Run the Processes

When you're ready to let 'er rip, click Run. Photoshop performs all the processes you've specified on the images you selected. Sit back and read a book, or go home early.

You'll find the final files in the folder you selected. ▥

Adding Watermarks

Protect your work and advertise your services by adding watermarks to your images with this often overlooked tool.

> **T I P**
>
> **Style Matters.** Many site styles in the Web Photo Gallery dialog restrict the image width to 450 pixels. For larger images, select a style with "horizontal" in its name. Horizontal images can be up to 1200 pixels wide.

1. Open Web Photo Gallery

I'm cheating a little here by using the Web Photo Gallery feature to create watermarks, even though for this project I am not going to use the resulting Web site.

First, select the images you want to watermark in Bridge. Then, choose Tools > Photoshop > Web Photo Gallery.

2. Customize the Watermark

Set the Destination and General Options for your files. Then, choose Security from the Options pop-up menu. This is where you'll make the watermark your own.

From the Content menu, choose Custom Text, and then type the text you want to use. Set the font and font size, color, opacity, position, and rotation. Essentially, your watermark can be as large as 72-point or as little as you like, and it can appear anywhere on the photograph.

Click OK to create the watermarked files. The Web Photo Gallery feature creates all the files required for a Web gallery, including an HTML file, navigation, graphics, and so on. The watermarked images are in the Images folder in your destination folder. You're finished! ▦

Adobe Camera Raw Essentials

Adobe Camera Raw (ACR) just keeps getting more powerful. Camera Raw 4 introduces new features that, for the first time, make it possible to do *all* your global editing in Camera Raw—without ever having to open Photoshop! Since you can now edit Raw, JPEG, or TIFF images in Camera Raw, it provides one-stop optimizing for most of your photos.

T I P

Before vs. After. To be able to compare original images with the ones you've modified in Camera Raw, duplicate the original before editing it: Select the image in the Content panel in Bridge, and choose Edit > Duplicate (or Command/Ctrl-D). Sort by filename in the Filter panel so that they appear next to each other in the Content panel. Do this multiple times if you would like to try variations.

Setting Preferences

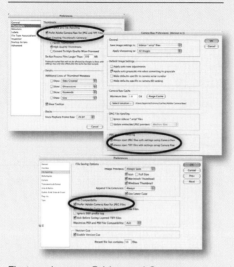

First, make sure Bridge and Camera Raw are speaking the same language. In Bridge, choose Edit > Preferences (Windows) or Bridge CS3 > Preferences (Mac OS), and then select Thumbnails in the list on the left. Select **Prefer Adobe Camera Raw For JPEGs And TIFF Files.** While you're in the Thumbnails pane, select High Quality Thumbnails to see accurate previews in Bridge of the work you do in Camera Raw.

Next, choose Edit > Camera Raw Preferences (Windows) or Bridge CS3 > Camera Raw Preferences (Mac OS). At the bottom of the dialog box, select **Always Open JPEG Files With Settings Using Camera Raw and Always Open TIFF Files With Settings Using Camera Raw.** With these selected, Camera Raw will read the metadata adjustments and apply them.

In Photoshop, choose Edit > Preferences (Windows) or Photoshop > Preferences (Mac OS) and select File Handling. Select **Prefer Adobe Camera Raw For JPEG Files** and **Prefer Adobe Camera Raw For Supported Raw Files** to have access to Camera Raw even if you open an image within Photoshop.

Opening Images in Camera Raw

In Bridge, select the images, and then choose File > Open In Camera Raw. (File > Open opens both Photoshop and Camera Raw.)

Camera Raw displays previews of the selected images in the **filmstrip** on the left side. The filmstrip only appears if you've opened more than one image. Because the filmstrip is the only place you'll see a **preview of a cropped image,** I recommend opening multiple images even if you're only going to work with one. If you select two or more images in the filmstrip, everything you do in the main area affects all the selected images.

The **Synchronize** button at the top of the filmstrip panel lets you quickly apply the same settings—such as crop settings, white balance adjustments, and so on—to other images. You can choose which attributes are synchronized.

Using the White Balance Tool

The White Balance tool is probably the most useful tool when you're working with images that were shot in raw format. In raw files, the camera settings are saved as metadata, not permanently applied to the image, so you can adjust the white balance in ACR as if it had been set correctly when the image was shot.

Select the White Balance tool, and then click within the image on a neutral gray (lighter is better than darker). Camera Raw automatically removes the color cast.

I recommend including something that you know to be a neutral gray in your shot, especially if you're shooting under artificial light. Then you'll know exactly what to click on with the White Balance tool.

You won't have quite the flexibility or quality with a JPEG image because the white balance setting in the camera is "cooked" into the file. ▶ **See page 158 for more on white balance.**

See page 158 for more on white balance.

> #### INSIGHT
>
> **Exposure Is the Exception.** Unlike the white balance, the camera's exposure setting is burned into even raw images. However, the contrast setting for raw files isn't, so images may have less clipping in shadows and highlights than "non-raw" files might have at the same exposure.

Cropping and Straightening

Two tools crop images in Camera Raw: the Crop tool **A** and the Straighten tool **B**. Use the Crop tool to create a rectangular crop with the same image orientation. Use the Straighten tool to rotate the image as you crop it—very useful if the image is skewed or tilted.

To crop an image, select the Crop tool, and then drag the area you want to use for your main composition. To use the Straighten tool, select it and drag along what you want to be horizontal or vertical.

An important feature of cropping is that it removes extraneous information that you don't want Camera Raw to use when making basic tonal corrections (such as using the **Auto** option). As you crop an image, the histogram changes to reflect only the data within the cropped area.

Retouching Images

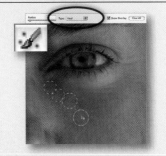

The Retouch tool combines the power of the Healing Brush tool in Photoshop and its Clone Stamp tool; you can use the Retouch tool in either mode. The Retouch tool was designed to remove dust spots that appear on an image when the sensor isn't clean, but it's an excellent tool for removing other minor anomalies as well.

Click the tool on the center of the anomaly you want to fix, and then drag it out to encompass the area. (The default radius of the area is one pixel but by dragging you can make it larger.) Here's the beautiful thing: The tool automatically looks for an area to use as a source for repairing the image. If you've used the Healing Brush and Clone Stamp tools in Photoshop, you know that you first have to select a source area for those fixes; in Camera Raw, simply click the area you want to fix. And if you're not happy with the source area Camera Raw chooses, you can move it.

As you work with the Retouch tool, Camera Raw displays the areas you've affected. Deselect Overlay to hide them (or tap the "V" key for View); the overlay is automatically hidden when you select another tool.

The Clone option copies **color, texture,** and **tone**; the Heal option, which is what you'll use nine times out of ten, only copies the *texture* area from the source, not the color or tone.

Making Basic Corrections

©JHDAVIS

The Basics panel contains the corrections sliders you'll use with most images. I've listed them here in the order I recommend using them. You'll find you get better and quicker results with less adjusting by working in this order.

▶ **See page 41 for a project that takes you through this process.**

1 Auto: The Auto option sets the white and black points for the image. It's a good place to start, but it usually creates an image that's a little too bright.

2 Brightness: Brightness affects the mid-tones, not the highlights or shadows, as in previous versions of Photoshop. (That also has been fixed in Photoshop CS3.) If you already set your black and white points by using Auto, then this midtone brightness adjustment may give you exactly what you are looking for in your image. If it doesn't, move on to the other sliders.

3 Contrast: Contrast also affects the midtones, so you can increase contrast without clipping highlights and shadows. The contrast gives an image its pop.

4 Fill Light: This slider affects the three-quarter tones, the bottom of the histogram. You can pull out an incredible amount of detail using this feature.

5 Recovery: Think of this as your quarter-tones slider. The top portion of the histogram can be controlled using the Recovery slider, bringing out more detail if you need it. You usually don't need the Recovery slider if you've set the exposure correctly.

6 Exposure: Use this to set the brightest white of the image if Auto didn't work well enough.

7 Blacks: Use this to set the darkest point in the image.

8 Clarity: At this stage you're ready to begin enhancing your image, since you've used the other sliders to optimize its tone. Introduced in Camera Raw 4.1, this slider provides localized contrast. It enhances edges that are inherent in the file. Typically, drag the Clarity slider up until you see a halo, then back off. It's ideal for landscapes, but be careful with portraits because it exaggerates skin blemishes.

9 Vibrance: Vibrance creates targeted saturation. It bumps up the saturation in portions of the image that aren't already saturated. Vibrance is more light-handed on the colors typically associated with skin tones: yellows, oranges, and browns. It's an effective method for increasing saturation without clipping detail by "pushing" already saturated colors.

10 Saturation: Saturation changes the overall saturation of the image. You may not need to use it if you can achieve the effect you want using the Vibrance slider. You may also want to use the two controls in combination for special effects: try increasing Saturation, then decreasing Vibrance to remove saturation in some areas.

Adjusting Curves

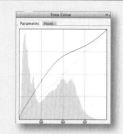

The Tone Curves panel gives you two ways to remap the tonality of an image: parametric curves and point curves. To modify parametric curves, move sliders to adjust highlights (the first quarter of the histogram), lights (the next quarter), darks, and shadows. You can even remap the tones by moving the control triangles at the base of the graph to adjust where the correction is taking place. You can change what is considered a highlight, light, dark, or shadow. *Parametric curves* provide an excellent simple method to adjust your image without fear of degrading it, because no matter how far you move a slider, the curve never folds back on itself, which would band or posterize or flatten the tone.

Point curves are completely separate from parametric curves. Start with parametric curves and if you still need more control, use point curves by clicking to create anchor points on the line and then dragging them up or down.

INSIGHT

Two Ways to See Clipping. Press Option/Alt as you drag the Exposure and Blacks sliders to see where clipping is occurring in your image. Click the triangle in the upper-left corner of the histogram to display clipping in the shadows, and the triangle in the upper-right corner to display clipping in the highlights.

Sharpening Images

The Detail tab gives you sharpening and noise-reduction controls. To preview changes you make on the Detail tab, you must zoom in on your image to at least 100%. (Double-click the magnifying glass icon to automatically go to 100%.)

There are four sharpening controls: Amount, Radius, Detail, and Masking. Generally, you'll get the best results if you start by moving the *Amount* slider up, exaggerating the sharpening effect so you can see what is being affected, then balance it out with other sliders and fine-tune the Amount back down. The pixel radius (*Radius* slider) ranges from .5 to 3. A larger Radius is useful for out-of-focus images because it exaggerates the halos around a soft edge. If your image is sharp, move the Radius as low as you can to minimize the likelihood of halo effects.

Detail is the amount of contrast on the edge based on the Radius. Increasing the Detail exaggerates the sharpening. Keep Detail as low as possible to avoid bringing in anomalies. A low Detail setting, say between 0 and 25, can emphasize the detail without pulling in too many artifacts.

The *Masking* slider is the cat's pajamas. It lets you restrict sharpening only to the edges. When you increase Masking,

subtleties in your image (such as noise and skin texture) are no longer exaggerated, but edges are still sharpened. Press Option/Alt to see the masking as you move the slider. At 0, everything is sharpened; as you move the slider to the right, less of your image is sharpened **A**.

If you're saving the image directly from Camera Raw, sharpen as much as necessary. However, if you'll be working with the image in Photoshop, keep the sharpening lower, but then sharpen again at the end of your workflow for a specific output.

Noise reduction can be tricky. Color noise is removed by blurring all the color detail in your file—detail you probably wanted to keep when you shot the image. Try setting the slider low, ideally down to 3, 4, or 5. Use the Luminance slider (which removes contrast noise) only if you really need it, but be careful because it can produce a watercolor effect.

> ### T I P
> **Preview as You Go.** Select and deselect the Preview button (or tap the P key) to compare what you have now with what you started with.

Modifying Saturation

The HSL/Grayscale panel provides a better set of features than anything in Photoshop for targeted hue, saturation, and luminance control.

For color images, there are three tabs: Hue, Saturation, and Luminance. Raw images have potentially billions of colors rather than millions in a JPEG file, and all of those subtleties come into play when you adjust these sliders.

While working in this tab, keep your eye on the histogram to make sure you're not clipping detail as you change color or tone.

For an interesting *colorized effect,* move all the Saturation sliders to the far left, so the image appears to be grayscale, and then saturate just one or two colors—like the colors of the flower petals above.

To truly convert an image to *grayscale,* click Convert To Grayscale at the top of the panel; a single tab is labeled Grayscale Mix. The sliders adjust the luminance of the components within the grayscale image. For example, you can lighten the orange skin tones in a grayscale image to de-emphasize blemishes.

Working with Other Panels

MODEL: NADINE ©JHDAVIS

Other panels in Camera Raw provide powerful tools for specific workflows. I'll talk more about some of these tools in later chapters.

Split Toning: This panel creates tinting effects. It's a powerful feature that lets you control where the color tone is applied in your image. I recommend increasing the Saturation value for the Shadows portion of your split-tone first, then moving the Hue slider to the color you like, and finally, using the Balance slider to set whether you get a lot of color or just a little in the midtones and highlights. I typically stay away from the Highlights slider, preferring instead to keep the light portions of the image clean. Remember, just because you *can* put green into a highlight doesn't mean you *should*.

Lens Correction: Use the **Lens Vignetting** feature to brighten up the dark edge of an image, or to purposely darken the edge slightly to draw the eye inward. To add vignetting, move the Amount slider to the left. The Midpoint determines how quickly the image transitions from regular tone to the added vignette.

Chromatic aberration is the typical blue/purple fringing that takes place in an image when light is bent inconsistently, especially if you're using a less-than-ideal wide-angle lens and shooting a scene with highly contrasted edges. Essentially, you use the sliders to scale or distort the red, green, and blue components back into alignment. (I also recommend that you slip "chromatic aberration" into your conversations whenever possible. It impresses clients.)

Camera Calibration: By photographing a custom color chart, like a Gretag Macbeth ColorChecker Chart, and then adjusting the file in ACR, you can use this feature to create a custom profile for your camera.

Presets: Save your settings and reapply them later. Or get a headstart using the presets I've included for you with this book.

▶ *Learn to use presets in a time-saving workflow in "Using Presets in a Camera Raw Workflow" on page 43.*

Saving Images

Before you finish adjusting your image in Camera Raw, set the workflow options, which include the color space, bit depth, resolution, and size. At the bottom of the window, a blue "link" displays a summary of the options; click the link to open the Workflow Options dialog box.

Select **Open In Photoshop As Smart Objects** as your default so that you can apply nondestructive smart filters and can edit the changes you made in Camera Raw at any time in the future. When this option is selected, the **Open Image** button changes to **Open Object.**

If your image doesn't need to be opened in Photoshop for further enhancing or retouching, save your image for use in other applications or for sending it out for print by clicking Save Image, selecting the file format (DNG, TIFF, JPEG, or PSD), destination, and file name.

©JHDAVIS

Editing Images in Camera Raw: An Accelerated Workflow

For most images, you can get great results with this simple, five-step workflow in Camera Raw.

▶ See Chapter 3 for a detailed step-by-step description of an accelerated workflow.

1. Set White Balance, Crop the Image

First, see page 37 for fixing color casts with the White Balance eyedropper. Second, before you make any adjustments, make sure that Camera Raw is considering only the pixels you actually want to use. For example, if you know you're going to remove an area of the sky that's blown out, crop it now. The histogram changes when you crop an image—and that means the settings for the adjustments you make will be different, too. Use the Crop tool ( ) for straightforward cropping; use the Straighten tool ( ) if you need to correct a skew or tilt in the image.

TIP

Clipping Revealed. Press the Option/Alt key while you're moving the Exposure or Blacks slider to see the clipped areas highlighted in the image window.

2. Set Black and White Points with Auto

Next, set the dynamic range of the image to be as bright and as dark as you want it to be. Start by choosing Auto for the White Balance in the Basic panel so that Camera Raw will automatically set the extremes of the white and black points. You may fine-tune these sliders now, but I recommend you wait until *after* your adjustments are completed, if necessary. You'll understand why in a moment!

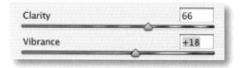

3. Adjust the Tonal Values

Now that you've set the ends of the range, you can concentrate on the midtone values. Typically you'll want to decrease the Brightness value to pull in more detail, and increase the Contrast value to give the image a little more punch. Depending on your image, try adjusting the Contrast before the Brightness.

If necessary, you can try pulling out shadow detail using the Fill Light slider, or use the Recovery slider to fine-tune the highlights.

4. Enhance the Image

The Clarity slider affects localized contrast. In most images, increasing the Clarity value helps bring out some apparent detail in the file. The exception is when you're editing a person or people in a portrait.

Be careful with the Clarity slider; if the value's too high, you can get a halo effect. Move the slider up until you see the halo, and then lower it slightly. Try increasing the Vibrance a little for a little extra "oomph."

▶ *See page 39 for more about sharpening.*

5. Sharpen the Details

Zoom your view to 100% and select the Detail icon. Move the Amount slider all the way up so you can see the results clearly during your adjustments. Now set the Radius: If your image is already in sharp focus, set Slider to below 1 pixel; if it's a little soft, set the slider to above 1 pixel. Next, to avoid creating artifacts, set the Detail slider as low as you can and keep the detail you want. Now, hold down the Option/Alt key as you move the Masking slider up; apply the mask just to the areas that have inherent contrast, where you really want the sharpening to occur. Finally, reduce your Amount slider to taste. Apply Noise reduction as needed after sharpening. ▦

Using Presets in a Camera Raw Workflow

For my readers and students I have created nearly 100 presets to streamline your work in Camera Raw. As you learn what works best for your images, you'll want to create your own presets, too. Basically, once you've performed a task, you should never have to do it again. With a preset, a quick click applies the change.

You can use presets to automate the Camera Raw workflow, and then apply these same adjustments to multiple images.

INSIGHT

How to Wow Presets. Go to www.adventuresinphotoshop. com and click on the How to Wow Presets link. This will take you to a special page on the OnOne Software site where you'll find Download links for installers for both Mac and Windows versions of my ACR and Lightroom Presets.

1. Set Preferences

If you haven't already, make sure Bridge, Camera Raw, and Photoshop all allow Camera Raw to open JPEG and TIFF files:

In Bridge, choose Edit > Preferences (Windows) or Bridge CS3 > Preferences (Mac OS), and select Thumbnails in the list on the left. **Select Prefer Adobe Camera Raw For JPEG And TIFF Files.** Select **High Quality Thumbnails** so that the previews in Bridge reflect changes made in Camera Raw. Select Cache (Windows) or Advanced (Mac OS) in the list, and select **Automatically Export Caches To Folders When Possible.** Exporting the cache ensures that the metadata travels with the file.

In Bridge, choose Edit > Camera Raw Preferences (Windows) or Bridge CS3 > Camera Raw Preferences (Mac OS). **Select Always Open JPEG Files With Settings Using Camera Raw and Always Open TIFF Files With Settings Using Camera Raw.**

In Photoshop, choose Edit > Preferences (Windows) or Photoshop > Preferences (Mac OS), and choose File Handling. Select **Prefer Adobe Camera Raw For JPEG Files** and **Prefer Adobe Camera Raw For Supported Raw Files.**

2. Open Images

In Bridge, select the images you want to edit, and double-click one of them. Camera Raw opens all the images, displaying them in the filmstrip on the left.

You can make all the changes you need for most images—from white balance to tone adjustments, split-toning to adding a vignette—using the How to Wow presets. Click the Presets icon to display the Presets panel.

Presets are listed in the order they're used in a typical workflow. Each preset begins with the word "Wow" and then a letter, which indicates its category:

a – white balance

b – tone adjustments

c – color settings

d – black-and-white conversion

e – old photo effects

f – desaturation

g – tinting

h – sharpening

For many images, these presets are all you'll need. But you may need to fine-tune some of the settings for more challenging images.

3. Set the White Balance

If your image appears to have a color cast (usually brought about by shooting under artificial lighting), set the white balance. First, click the Auto **(WOW-a_WB-Auto)** preset; it's as if you clicked Auto in the Basic panel. Camera Raw attempts to reset the color temperature for the image. Click each of the other white balance presets to see the adjustment effect applied to your image. You can click through the presets quickly, experimenting with settings you might never have considered otherwise—and it's all completely nondestructive. You can't hurt anything using the presets, so have some fun.

INSIGHT

Use Presets in Bridge. You can apply these presets without even opening images in Camera Raw. In Bridge, right-click (Windows) or Control-click (Mac OS) an image, choose Develop Settings, and then select the preset. Use the same workflow: set the white balance first and proceed through the categories.

You can copy settings from one file to another in Bridge, too: right-click or Control-click the first image, and choose Develop Settings > Copy Settings; then right-click or Control-click the second image, and choose Develop Settings > Paste Settings.

---

4. Adjust the Tone

After you've set the white balance, move on to tonal adjustments. Always start with the **Auto-Tone-Set First** preset. (There's a reason I put "Set First" in the name, after all.) This preset takes advantage of Camera Raw's ability to automatically set the white and black points for the image. Then you can apply a brightness preset to add or remove brightness as necessary. For example, the Brit_0 preset sets the brightness to 0, and Brit_+50 sets it to 50. The presets that include "+C" add contrast.

The Tone-Salvage setting is a good way to see exactly how much information is in a dark image, especially when you're trying to determine whether to keep an image or not. And, you can apply this adjustment in the Bridge where you're resorting images, without even opening Camera Raw *(see the Insight on this page)*.

5. Apply Color Settings

The color presets include Vibrance and Saturation options. Vibrance is a variation on Saturation; it increases or decreases saturation in a nonlinear fashion. You can add or remove Vibrance, or combine it with Saturation, as is the case with the preset that performs the extreme saturation boost, called "Vibrance +4."

The How to Wow HSL presets are related to skin and sky, so that you can isolate skin tones and then increase the luminance. By making the image lighter, you can often minimize anomalies such as freckles, rosacea, and razor burn. I use generic orange as the basic skin tone color, which works for all ethnicities. Some skin tones are more yellow or brown, but still within the range of oranges.

The HSL Desat preset appears to create a black-and-white version of the image, but it actually just moves the Saturation values of each color to −100. Don't use it to create black-and-white images, but it's a great starting point if you want to resaturate specific colors to create a neat colorized effect.

► *See page 162 for a project utilizing this technique.*

6. Add Effects

©JHDAVIS

The next four sets of presets create special photographic effects. For example, use the black-and-white effects if you want to create a black-and-white image.

There are several tint presets you can play with to get some very interesting variations on a sepia or cyan tint.

Use presets to create vignettes, which you can use to draw the eye into the center of the image—or to lighten a vignette that exists in the original image.

If you want to give your photo an antique effect, try applying one of the **Effect_Old_ Photo** presets.

▶ *For more on enhancing in ACR, see Chapter 12, "Enhancing Images in Camera Raw," beginning on page 157.*

7. Sharpen

After you've made all the other changes, sharpen the image. Remember that Camera Raw only displays the effects of sharpening if you're viewing the image at 100% or higher. You cannot preview sharpening at lower percentages.

I've included a range of sharpening presets. Use the one appropriate for your image. There are presets for **Landscapes** and **Portraits**. The Portrait presets have higher masking values to protect skin tones from being overly sharpened. Use the light sharpening preset (WOW-h_ Sharpen_Portrait Lt) for an image that's already in pretty good shape; use heavy-plus (WOW-h_Sharpen_Portrait Hvt) if you really need to sharpen up a blurry photo. All my presets use masking to restrict the areas that are being sharpened (areas with natural contrast).

8. Synchronize

When you've applied one or more presets, and you're happy with the image, apply the same settings to similar images instantly. Select the images in the filmstrip in Camera Raw, and click Synchronize. In the Synchronize dialog box, you can choose which settings to copy.

You can also save the settings as a new preset, which can be especially useful if you find you want to apply the same combination of presets to other photographs at a later time. To save a preset, click the New Preset icon (⊞) at the bottom of the Presets panel. Select which settings you want to include, and click Save; in the Save dialog box, give the preset a name you'll understand later. All the How to Wow presets begin with the letter "W," so almost any new preset you save will appear above them in the Presets panel. ▥

CHAPTER 3
Smart Nondestructive Workflow

© J. DAVIS

HARM NO PIXELS, keep all options, waste no steps. Procedural processing (adjusting an image by recording the values of multiple of sliders, rather than the manipulation of millions of individual pixels) gives you true flexibility when shaping an image. Combine the tried and true procedural technologies such as Adjustment Layers and Layer Styles with the capabilities of Adobe's newest nondestructive lifesaver, Smart Filters, and you have a quiver of creative arrows to target the most challenging jobs.

MODEL: DONNA ©JHDAVIS

Global Editing in Camera Raw

Since you can edit TIFF, JPEG, and raw images nondestructively, it makes sense to do most of your global editing in Camera Raw from now on!

1. Set the White Balance

Click on the image in Bridge and press Command/Ctrl-R to open it in Camera Raw. Then select the White Balance tool (🖌) and click on an area that should be a neutral gray (a white wall, for instance) to neutralize any color cast. If there are no neutrals, adjust the White Balance menu and Temperature and Tint sliders to your liking.

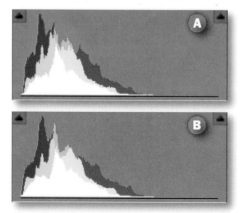

2. Crop and Straighten the Image

When you adjust the tone, Camera Raw ignores all the data outside the cropped area. So if you plan to crop the image anyway, do it now. Even commitment-phobes can crop with confidence because the changes are nondestructive; you can always uncrop later. Use the Crop tool (🔲) to crop the image; use the Straighten tool (📐) to crop and rotate it at the same time. Notice that the histogram changes from the original **A** to reflect the data inside the cropped area **B**.

▶ **See page 37 for more on White Balance.**

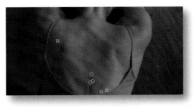

3. Retouch as Necessary

If there are distractions (blemishes, dust, or spots, for instance) in your image, fix them with the Retouch tool (). Heal mode is most useful 90% of the time, but you can also use the tool in Clone mode.

4. Make Tonal Adjustments

Even if you plan to convert an image to grayscale, the correct tonal range needs to be set first. Make changes in the middle section of the Basic panel. Click the Auto button to let Camera Raw set the dynamic range for the image, and then adjust the sliders for Brightness, Contrast, Fill Light, Recovery, Exposure, and Blacks (in that order) to optimize the tone for the story you're telling. Unless the image is a portrait, try adjusting the Clarity slider to increase the edge contrast.

5. Adjust Other Settings

Next convert this image to grayscale using the HSL/Grayscale panel, and then fine-tune the tonality if needed.

To give this image a sepia tone, spend some time in the Split Toning panel. First, work with the shadows, adjusting Hue and Saturation, then move the Balance slider to keep the highlights more neutral.

Next stop is the Lens Corrections tab to add a vignette that draws the eye into the center of the composition. Lower the Amount slider all the way, but move the midpoint up a bit.

6. Open the Smart Object

When you've made global changes, move on to more targeted editing in Photoshop. Make sure the workflow settings at the bottom of the Camera Raw window fit your needs; click the link to change the settings. Then click Open Object to open the image as a Smart Object in Photoshop. ▦

Working with Smart Filters

Move into Photoshop to perform *targeted* (as opposed to *global*) adjustments—retouching, optimizing, or enhancing the image. Smart Filters, which apply changes nondestructively, combine the power of filters with the flexibility of Adjustment Layers and the target precision of masks.

About Smart Filters

Smart Filters, introduced in Photoshop CS3, are Photoshop filters applied to Smart Objects. You can create the same effects you ordinarily create with the filters, but the changes are nondestructive: You can readjust, remove, or hide the filters at any time.

The key is to make sure you're working with a Smart Object. That's why you selected **Open In Photoshop As Smart Objects** in the Workflow Options dialog box in Camera Raw.

Almost any filter in the Filter menu can be used as a Smart Filter. The exceptions include Extract, Liquify, Pattern Maker, Vanishing Point, and Lens Blur. The name "Smart Filter" is a little misleading, because you can also apply the Shadow/ Highlight and Variations adjustments as Smart Filters.

Applying Smart Filter Effects

You apply Smart Filters the same way you apply any other filter in Photoshop. Start by selecting the layer you want to modify. Then, choose a filter from the Filter menu. If the selected layer is a Smart Object, the filter you select is automatically a Smart Filter. For this image, we'll use the Surface Blur effect to soften the distractions of the floor and other people in the shot.

In the filter effects dialog box, adjust the settings for your image. Click in the preview window to see the image before the effect is applied, and then release the mouse to see a preview of the effect.

When you're happy with the filter settings, click OK. The Smart Filter appears below the Smart Object layer. You can turn the filter on or off, change its opacity, or change the blending mode.

When you apply a Smart Filter, a mask is automatically available to let you easily mask the filter effects.

To see all the Smart Filters applied to a layer, click the triangle next to the Smart Filter icon, to the right of the Smart Object layer in the Layers palette. Click the triangle again to hide the filters and keep the Layers palette tidy.

Masking Smart Filter Effects

When applying a filter to a Smart Object, a mask thumbnail appears in the Layers palette **A**. If you've made a selection before applying the filter, the mask reflects that; otherwise, it reveals the entire filter effect.

Use the mask to selectively mask the effects of the Smart Filter. Filter masks are similar to layer masks, and you can work with them the same way. When you paint on a filter mask, areas that you paint in black hide the effect and areas in white reveal the effect; gray areas moderate the effect. There's one drawback: The masking applies to all Smart Filters applied to the Smart Object; you can't mask individual filters.

To paint on the mask, choose the Brush tool and set its Opacity. For this image, I used a 250-pixel slightly hard brush with an opacity of 75%. Where I painted black, the sharpness of the original returned. Because the story of this image is the position of the toes and the muscular back of the Yogin, I focused on those areas. Then I reduced the Opacity to 25%, and reduced the brush size, and painted the rest of the model, bringing nearby areas into partial focus.

Remember that black areas hide and white areas reveal; to remove some of the mask, paint with white.

To see the mask without the image behind it **B**, press Option/Alt and click the mask in the Layers palette. You can paint on the mask itself while you're viewing it, filling in unintentional gaps, softening transitions. You can even run a filter on a mask.

Unlike layer masks, filter masks aren't linked to layers. If you move either a filter mask or a layer using the Move tool, they do not move together.

To move the mask to another Smart Filter effect, drag it. To copy the mask, Option/Alt-drag it to another Smart Filter effect.

To disable a filter mask, Shift-click its thumbnail in the Layers palette, or choose Layer > Smart Filter > Disable Filter Mask. The mask has a red X over it when it's disabled. To enable the mask, Shift-click its thumbnail again.

Selecting Variations

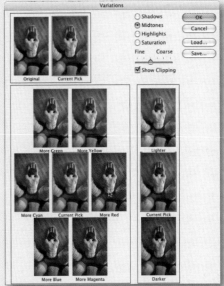

Smart Filters include some items that aren't even filters. For example, for the first time, you can apply Variations adjustments nondestructively.

Select the Smart Object layer itself, not the mask. Then choose Image > Adjustments > Variations. The Variations dialog box shows you different color options and lighter or darker options. Use sliders to make adjustments to highlights, midtones, or shadows. You can even show clipping. The original and current picture are displayed in the upper-left corner.

For this image, I selected Highlights so that when I clicked on the Darker thumbnail, I wouldn't clip the shadow areas. The filter mask ensures that the change applies only to the area that is not masked, so I could darken the highlights in the floor without affecting the highlights in the subject.

Using Layer Styles

Another example of a nondestructive procedural manipulation technology available in Photoshop is our beloved Layer Style effects. And as with Smart Filters, you can add as many effects as you want (they're all nondestructive), change your mind, or share the effects with other images at any time.

About Layer Styles

A Layer Style is an effect or set of effects applied to a layer. The layer effect applied by a Layer Style, such as shadows or bevels, are linked to the layer contents. For example, if you apply a drop shadow to a text layer and then edit the text, the drop shadow is reapplied to conform to the new text.

As with Smart Filters, layer styles are nondestructive because you can turn them on or off, or edit them even after they're applied. You can apply one of the Layer Styles presets that comes with Photoshop, or create a custom style using the Layer Style dialog box.

Adding Layer Styles

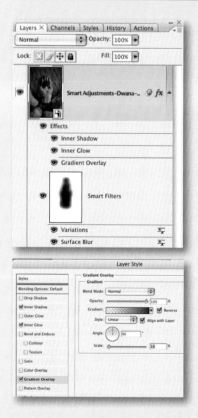

To add a Layer Style, select the layer, then click the Layers Styles icon (*fx.*) at the bottom of the Layers palette, and choose the effect you want to apply. Then you can change the settings in the Layer Style dialog box. Add other effects to the Style by clicking the check box to the left of an effect name. In fact, you can edit multiple effects without closing the Layer Style dialog box. Click an effect's name to edit its options.

For this image, I applied the Inner Shadow effect to continue to draw the eye in to the center of the image—but I set the Distance to 0 so there wouldn't actually be a directional shadow, just exaggerated edge vignetting. Since I wanted an even darker edge-framing effect, I cheated and I added an Inner Glow, and changed the color to black and the blending mode to Overlay. The Inner Glow effect further darkened the edge, creating the final framing effect.

To draw the eye to focus on the feet in the image, I applied Gradient Overlay and changed the default **Black to White** gradient to a **Foreground to Transparent** gradient. Then I changed the scale so that the transition from black to transparent would be quick, and I reversed and repositioned the gradient to get exactly the darkening I wanted at the top of the file. ▶ **See page 174 for a project about how to create a gradient overlay effect using Fill layers.**

All the changes I made are stored in the Layer Style, and the effects are listed under the layer. They'll travel with the layer, but I can change any of the settings or remove any of the effects at any time. ▥

Sharing Settings

After you've completed all the work on your image, you can share the same Smart Filter or Layer Styles with other files by simply dragging and dropping.

T I P

Share a Copy. Share your image without compromising your original PSD file. In Photoshop, choose Image > Duplicate. Then, in the copy, click the upper-right corner of the Layers palette, and choose Flatten Image. Now you can save the file in any format for the Web or other destination without worrying that anyone can alter any of your settings.

T I P

Copying Camera Raw Settings in Bridge. You can quickly copy changes you made in Camera Raw to another image. In Bridge, right-click the image you modified, and choose Develop Settings > Copy Settings. Then right-click another image, and choose Develop Settings > Paste Settings. Paste all the settings, or just a few.

Sharing Smart Filters

My philosophy is that wherever possible, you should only have to perform a task once. So, after you've set up a Smart Filter "recipe" that you like, use it on other images. To share the Smart Filters, drag the word "Smart Filters" from the Layers palette in the source document onto a Smart Object layer in the new image. If you're copying it from one layer to another within the same document, press Option/Alt as you drag. You'll probably have to edit the mask for the new image (like we did with the Buddha), but you'll save the steps of applying the filter and selecting its settings.

Sharing Layer Styles

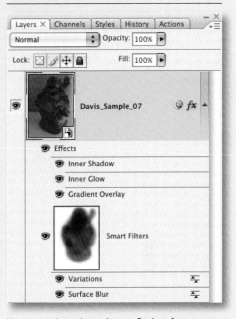

You can also share Layer Styles from one image to another. Click the word "Effects" and drag it onto another image. Remember that you can easily edit a Layer Style, so after you've copied it, you can hide or edit individual effects.

Another way of sharing a Layer Style is to save it as a preset. To save it, select the layer that contains the style, and then choose New Style from the menu in the upper-right corner of the Styles palette. Name the style, set options for it, and click OK. To apply it to a new image, select the layer and click the style in the Styles palette. Also, you can right-click on the layer that has a style and select *Copy Layer Style.* Then select another layer, right-click again, and choose *Paste Layer Style.*

CHAPTER 4
Selection Tips and Techniques

ONE OF THE FOUNDATIONAL tenets of working in computer graphics is: **Select Before You Manipulate.** (The other two tenets, of course, are **Save Often** and **Never Borrow Money Needlessly**.)

So how can you expedite this potentially laborious selection process so as to take advantage of Adobe programmers' genius and your computer's computational prowess?

In this chapter we will use selection tools and technologies that help streamline the process and increase the quality of the results: Quick Select, Refine Edge, and Blend Modes, as well as the oft overlooked but powerful Color Range and Background Eraser.

©JHDAVIS

Quick Select, Refine Edge, and Masking Secrets

The new Quick Selection tool is as good as its name. Use it in conjunction with the Refine Edge feature to quickly and accurately make selections.

1. Make an Initial Selection

Making an accurate selection is the first step to doing just about any of the really cool things Photoshop is capable of. The Quick Selection tool is smart enough to know what you're trying to do, so it can make complicated selections—such as the one in this image, which requires selecting around skin, hair, and a tiara—quickly.

Select the Quick Selection tool (✎) in the Tools palette (sometimes hidden under the Magic Wand tool). Then click and drag within the area you want to select. By default, the tool adds to the selection, so you can click additional areas to include them. To remove an area, select Subtract From Selection in the Options bar, or press Option/Alt as you click on the background. You can quickly get a fairly accurate selection—it doesn't have to be perfect just yet. But, deselect at least a little of the area in each hole, where the background peeks through.

2. Refine the Selection

The nifty new Refine Edge feature lets you clean up a selection efficiently. Click Refine Edge in the Options bar (available whenever any selection tool is active). To get started, click Default in the Refine Edge dialog box.

Radius and Contrast are the stars of this dialog box, because they aren't available elsewhere. The Radius setting determines where Photoshop looks for the edge. To pull in wispy hair, increase the Radius; for an image with hard-edged transitions, keep the Radius lower.

Contrast removes subtleties and halos that can appear when the Radius is too high. The trick is to strike a balance between getting the edges you want and avoiding the subtleties you don't want.

Use other sliders to fine-tune the balance. Smooth, Feather, and Contract/Expand all remove from and add to the selection. For fine detail, try setting your Smooth and Feather as low as possible, and then Contract to taste.

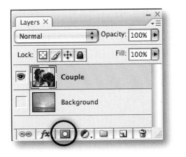

3. Create the Layer Mask

To use this selection to create a layer mask to further fine-tune the edge, click the Add Layer Mask icon in the Layers palette. The area outside the layer mask becomes transparent, revealing the background layers beneath it. In this case, a sunset appears behind the happy couple.

Clean up the mask using the Paintbrush (🖌) or the Dodge (🔍) and the Burn (✋) tools.

Use the Burn tool to darken and the Dodge tool to lighten. When *Range is set to Shadows, the Burn tool affects only dark grays;* when *Range is set to Highlights, the Dodge tool affects only light grays,* which is very useful for contracting and expanding specific areas of a mask!

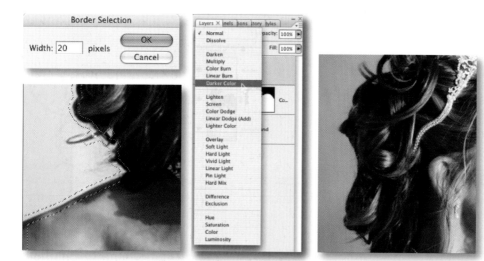

4. Use a Border to Capture Subtleties

When working with wispy hair, fringe, or other intricate edges in your selection, creating a separate border layer that contains the subtleties can help you capture the detail without spending hours at the task. Ctrl-click (Windows) or Command-click (Mac OS) the layer mask in the Layers palette to load the selection again. The marching ants reappear. Next, choose Select > Modify > Border. Select a width that will catch the stray bits of your selection; a 20-pixel width means that the border includes 10 pixels inside the selection and 10 pixels outside it.

To copy the border to its own layer, with the color portion of the layer active (not the mask), choose Layer > New > Layer Via Copy. Now here's the trick that makes this useful: Apply a blending mode that captures the detail you want in the border but doesn't include the background tones. Two new blending modes are ideal for this purpose: choose Darker Color if you want to keep the darker areas (that is, if the area you want to hide in the border is a lighter color), and choose Lighter Color if the area you want to keep is lighter.

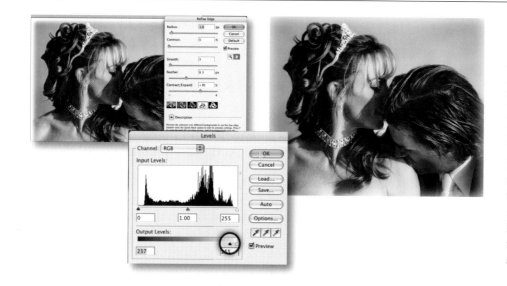

5. Add a Vignette

To finish up an image, you may also use a refined selection to add a vignette. Use the Marquee tool (⬚) to draw a rectangle just within the edges of the image, with Feather set to 0. Then click Refine Edge and enter a Feather value. When you like the previewed results, click OK. Then, choose Select > Inverse to invert the selection so that you're selecting the area outside of the rectangle, rather than the image within it. Finally, click the Add Adjustment Layer icon (⬤) in the Layers palette, choose a Levels adjustment layer, and move the black output slider to the right. ▥

© JHDAVIS

Selecting by Color Range

Specify a color range to isolate skin tones (to soften them while keeping facial details sharp) or other areas that are difficult to select.

1. Open as a Smart Object

Open the image in Camera Raw. It's the best place to make global edits, and it lets you take the image directly into Photoshop as a Smart Object.

Set the black and white points, adjust the midtones, and make any other changes you need to make. Then open the image in Photoshop as a Smart Object: Click the Open Object button or if the button says Open Image, press the Shift key to change it to Open Object.

2. Make the Initial Selection

Use the good old-fashioned Lasso tool (○) to make a rough selection around the area you want to focus on—in this case, the model's skin. Set Feather to 50 and make a soft selection around the entire face. If you're selecting something with hard, geometric edges, use the Pen tool (✐) to make the first selection.

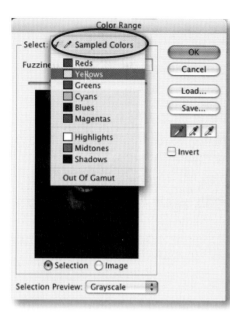

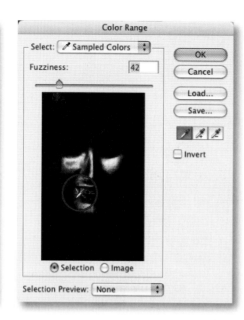

3. Select the Color Range

Choose Select > Color Range. The Color Range command selects a color or color range within an entire image, or within an existing selection.

In the Color Range dialog box, you can select one of the reflected or emitted primary colors: red, green, blue, yellow, cyan, and magenta. You can also select highlights, midtones, or shadows. Most often, though, you'll want to select the colors in the image yourself. Select Sampled Colors, and then click areas of color on the preview image or on the full image.

By default, there is no preview. Choose Grayscale from the Selection Preview menu to get a clearer picture of your selection.

Use the eyedroppers in the dialog box to add to or subtract from the selection.

The Fuzziness slider determines how wide a range of colors is selected, and therefore how smoothly or abruptly Photoshop transitions from selected to nonselected pixels. When the slider is set to 0, only the precise colors you click are selected; that's called a one-bit transition. For most images, you'll want to set the Fuzziness slider to a value between 35 and 50 to make sure you catch similar colors, providing smoother transitions between what's selected and what's not.

Click OK when you're happy with the selection. You'll have the opportunity to clean it up a little more if you want to.

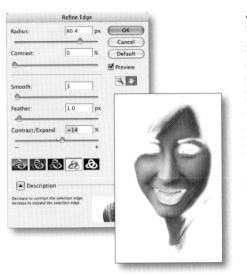

4. Refine the Selection

You could go right ahead and apply a filter now, but in Photoshop CS3, you always have the option of fine-tuning your selection first. Click the Refine Edge button in the Options bar, or choose Select > Refine Edge.

In the Refine Edge dialog box, click Default first to let it take a stab at smoothing the edges. Evaluate the results, and make any necessary adjustments. For example, you can increase the Radius value to soften the edge a little more. You might also want to adjust the Contract/Expand slider. Click OK when you're satisfied with the results.

5. Apply a Filter

With the selection in good shape, you're ready to apply a filter. Because the image is a Smart Object, any filter you apply is a nondestructive Smart Filter. The selection automatically becomes the filter mask, so the filter affects only the selected area.

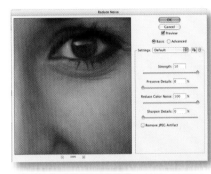

For this image, use the Reduce Noise filter to soften the skin tone. Choose Filter > Noise > Reduce Noise. Notice that the preview isn't completely accurate, because the filter mask hasn't been applied yet. But the filter does a nice job of softening the skin, especially pore details and subtleties. It leaves the areas with inherent contrast, such as eyes, teeth, and hair, as sharp as possible. Click OK to accept the filter settings. Now the filter mask appears in the Layers palette with the Smart Filter **A**.

To double the effect, run the filter again: Option/Alt-click the name of the Smart Filter, then drag it up until you see another line **B**.

You can also change the opacity and blending mode to modify the effect **C**, by clicking the sliders icon to the right of the filter's name. ▥

©JHDAVIS

Erasing a Background

Remove a background (while protecting your subject) with a few swipes of the Background Eraser tool, and then pop in any background you like.

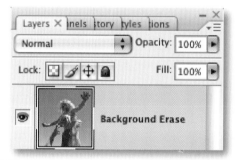

1. Copy the Content onto a New Layer

To work nondestructively, copy all the visible content from the existing layers onto a new layer. Press Command-Option-Shift-E (Mac OS) or Ctrl-Alt-Shift-E (Windows) to create the new layer. Name it Background Erase.

Hide all the other layers so you can see what's occurring.

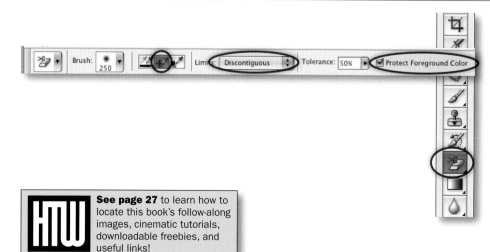

2. Set Up the Background Eraser

Select the Background Eraser tool, which is grouped with the Eraser tool. In the Options bar, select the Sampling: Once icon so that only the colors you specifically click are erased. From the Limits menu, choose Discontiguous so that the background pixels don't all have to touch to be erased. This is important when you're removing background around hair, for instance, where the background appears through gaps in the main image. The default tolerance of 50% is fine, but turn on Protect Foreground Color to retain control over what is *not* being erased.

See page 27 to learn how to locate this book's follow-along images, cinematic tutorials, downloadable freebies, and useful links!

3. Erase the Background

To select the color you want to protect you can quickly turn the tool into the eyedropper by Option/Alt-clicking on the color you want to safeguard, such as the blond-blue area in the girl's hair in this image.

Now, just paint over the background color you want to erase and it disappears. If there are multiple colors in the background, click in each color to start again. You can sample new foreground colors by Option/Alt-clicking on them to protect as you work your way around the image.

4. Insert a New Background

To see clearly how well you removed the background, insert a new one: Open another image in Photoshop and drop it into position in the Layers palette, beneath the existing layer. A generic photo of wispy clouds is always nice. Scale the image to fill the background. Double-click to set it in place.

TIP

Intensify Fine Lines. If wispy hairs are getting lost in the new background, double their effect. Use the Lasso tool with a feather of 10 pixels to select the rough area, and press Command/Ctrl-J to copy the selection to its own layer. Transparent or opaque areas are not affected, but subtleties are doubled.

5. Tidy Up

If there's a halo around the subject of your image, or if bits of the old background still appear, use the Background Eraser to continue sampling around the area. Reduce the size of the brush, protect the color in your subject, and then click a new area to erase and paint over the edge to clean it up. ▦

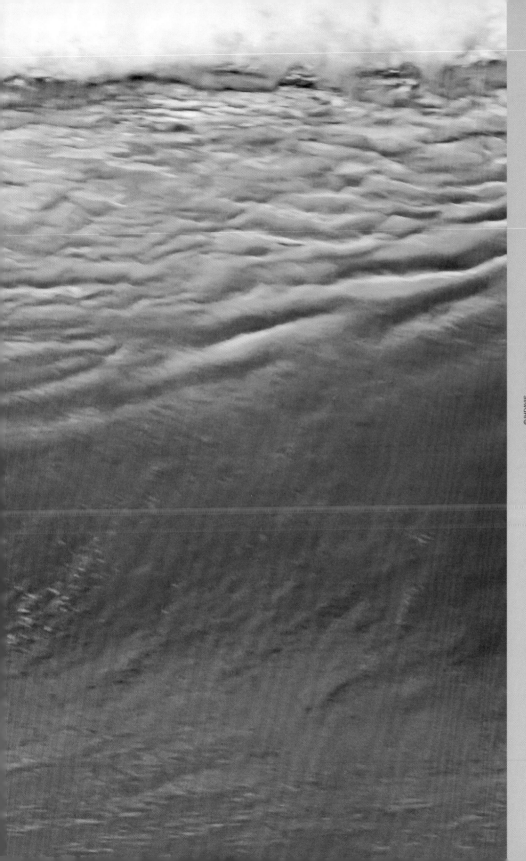

CHAPTER 5
Color and Tone Optimizing

©JHDAVIS

WITH MOST of our global adjustments and optimizations completed in Camera Raw, we now move onto *targeted tweaking* of the color and tonal range of our images from within Photoshop proper.

The established workhorse Curves, in conjunction with several Dodge and Burn techniques, will allow us to massage both the color and the tonal range in order to bring out the subtleties of our photographs, which can help to better convey each one's story.

And if one image just isn't enough to capture a scene to its fullest, we'll show you how to quickly combine multiple exposures into one high-quality masterpiece, but still retain creative flexibility within the file.

Using Curves to Fix Tone and Color

Use Curves to fix the tonality and the color of flattened, antique, or other less-than-optimal images.

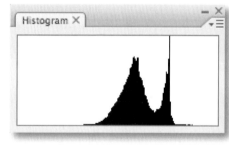

> Histogram ✕

INSIGHT

Manually Moving Curves. In the enhanced Curves dialog box, you can easily set the black and white points manually by moving in the black and white triangles with reference to the histogram. In the past, you could only do that in the Levels dialog box.

1. Open the Image

In the past, we relied on both the Levels and the Curves dialog boxes to adjust tone, but with Photoshop CS3, the Curves dialog box does it all. This image of a mannequin was shot through a plate-glass window, so the tone is flattened because of reflections from the sky. The Curves dialog box provides all the tools you need to bring it to life, so to speak.

Open the image in Photoshop, and make sure the Histogram palette is open and visible. You'll refer to the Histogram palette to see the changes in tonal range as you make adjustments in the Curves dialog box. To open the Histogram palette, choose Window > Histogram.

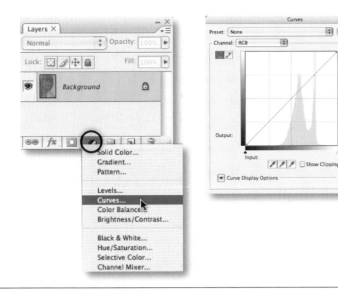

2. Create a Curves Adjustment Layer

Click the Create New Adjustment Layer icon at the bottom of the Layers palette, and choose Curves.

It's good practice to always make tonal and color adjustments using Adjustment Layers, which are nondestructive. You could open the Curves dialog box from the Image > Adjustment menu, but then any changes you made would permanently affect your original pixels.

The histogram in the Curves dialog box always displays the original tonality of the image. To see changes as you work in the dialog box, remember to refer to the Histogram palette you opened in step 1.

3. Set Up the Auto Feature

Click Auto. For many images, you'll see dramatic changes right away. How the tone changes depends on the settings in the Auto Color Correction Options dialog box. Click Options to see them.

By default, Enhance Per Channel Contrast is selected. It sets the black and white points for each of the independent red, green, and blue channels separately to remove a color cast. The Find Dark & Light Colors option is similar, but it uses the darkest dark and the lightest light in each channel to determine the settings. For some images, you might prefer Enhance Monochromatic Contrast, which sets one black and one white point for the entire image, and thus does not change the color.

Snap Neutral Midtones finds a nearly neutral color and adjusts the midtone values to make the color neutral. I like to minimize clipping as much as possible, so I typically set both at .01% (one-hundredth of one percent).

For this image, Find Dark & Light Colors paired with Snap Neutral Midtones gives the best results. Click OK to return to the Curves dialog box.

INSIGHT

Changing the Display. You can modify the Curves display to show grid or intersection lines, show amount of light or amount of pigment or ink, and other options. Click Curve Display Options to see your choices.

TIP

Using the Eyedropper in Curves. The sample size settings for the Eyedropper Tool at the bottom of the Tools palette affect how the eyedropper works in Curves. Set the Sample Size to 11 x 11 to increase the accuracy of their adjustments.

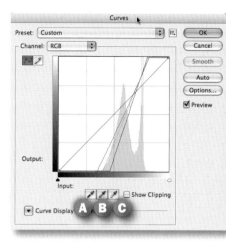

4. Remove Any Color Cast

You may need to move beyond Auto settings to achieve the tone you want. The eyedroppers set the black point **A**, the white balance **B**, and the white point **C**, respectively. Most useful for color correction is the middle one. Click on what should be a neutral area to remove a color cast without changing the tonality: It balances out the red, green, and blue based on what you identify as neutral. You can click around to see the effect as you search for areas that might work. You can't break anything by doing this, so take a few minutes to try different areas to see what gives you the best results.

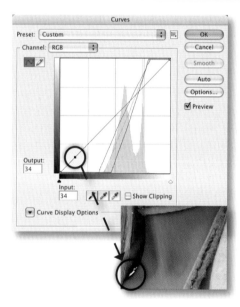

5. Protect the Curves

To fine-tune the tone, manipulate the curves themselves. First, *deselect* any eyedroppers so you won't accidentally reset the white balance. Then, move the cursor over the image. The eyedropper picks up information about the image beneath it, and shows you where that particular tonal range lies on the curve.

Before you make any changes to the curve, protect areas that are already where you want them. For example, in this image, the shadows by the mannequin's neck look like the darkest part of the image. To protect that portion of the tonal range, Command/Ctrl-click it to set an anchor point.

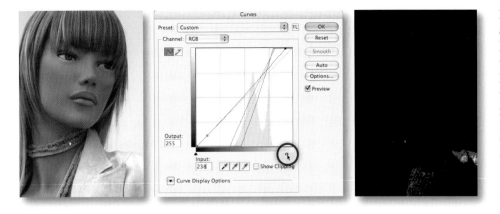

For protecting the highlights area, another technique was employed to help locate where the lightest spot in the photograph is located. To do this, hold down the Option/Alt key and drag the white triangle slider in the lower right of the Curves main square to the left. Option/Alt switches the preview to Threshold mode, which shows exactly where clipping is taking place. In this case, we can see the shoulder of the jacket is the lightest. Now move the slider back to the right, let go of the Option/Alt key, and Command/Ctrl-click on that area to set an anchor point.

6. Modify the Curve

To modify the curve, Command/Ctrl-click an area you want to change. That sets a point just as before, but this time we want to move it. Press the up or down arrow keys or drag the point manually to adjust the curve. Because the other points you set will remain in position to anchor the curve, you can increase the contrast without plugging up highlights or shadows. You can also create a point by clicking directly on the curve. Keep in mind that a steeper curve increases contrast; the more horizontal a curve, the flatter the tone. ▣

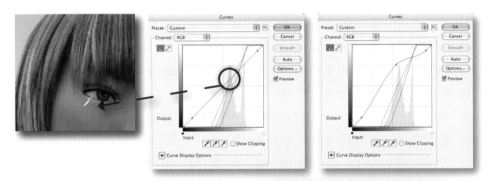

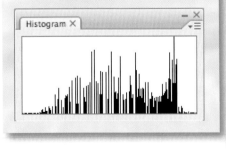

"Combing" vs. Smooth. Because this image was shot with a pocket camera in JPEG format, "combing" occurs when the dynamic range increases. Raw images have billions of potential colors, so combing doesn't occur with them.

©JHDAVIS

Targeting Tonal Adjustments with Curves

What can you do when part of your image has one tone and part has another? Use Curves and a mask to bring the two together.

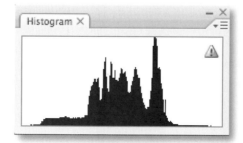

Histogram ✕

1. Select the Focus Area

This image poses an interesting challenge because part of a building is reflected in the window in front of the mannequins. From the histogram, you can tell that the photo already has a fairly complete dynamic range, with a substantial amount of shadow detail. So simply applying the Auto setting in the Curves dialog box, as in the last project, won't make much difference here. Instead, in a case like this, select the part of the image that is most important to the story you're trying to tell. You can use the Marquee tool or the Lasso tool, whatever makes sense for the area you're selecting. You'll adjust the curves for that part of the image, and then bring along the rest of the image later.

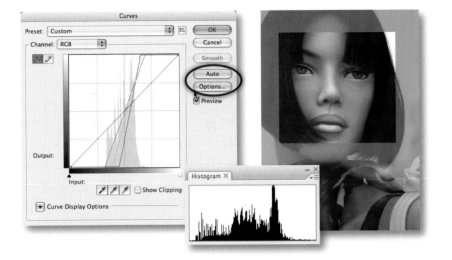

2. Adjust the Curves

Click the Create New Adjustment Layer icon at the bottom of the Layers palette, and choose Curves. The selected area is the only area that Photoshop will consider as it makes adjustments. Click Auto, then Options. As in the previous project, this image looks best with Find Dark & Light Colors and Snap Neutral Midtones selected. Once again, reduce the clipping to .01% to minimize clipping in both the highlights and the shadows.

You can make other changes, including setting the white point or white balance, or fine-tuning the actual curves.

3. Fill the Mask

The selected part of the image looks great, but unless you're planning to crop to only that part of it, you'll want to unmask the rest of the image. The entire image should reflect the settings in the selected area. One way to do that is to make sure the mask is selected, and then press Shift-Delete and choose Use White. The changes you made in the Curves dialog box now apply to the entire image.

4. Target the Effect

So far, so good, but the reflected area is still more intense than the face. It's time to make use of the mask in a different way now. Layers always come along with adjustment masks, just sitting there waiting for you to use them. Select the mask, get a big soft Brush, set at about 50% opacity, and paint wherever the Curves adjustments created too much intensity. The goal is for the lower portion of the image to match the upper areas for a more consistent look. ▥

MODEL: DEWITT JONES ©JHDAVIS

Smart Dodging and Burning

A single blending mode trick lets you nondestructively dodge and burn both highlights and shadows on the same layer.

1. Open the Image in Photoshop

One of the easiest ways to perform targeted tonal control (known as dodging and burning) is also one of my favorites. There's no need to spend time in Camera Raw or to work with a Smart Object *if this is all you're doing*, so you can open the image directly in Photoshop.

I N S I G H T

Take Your Pick. I'm showing you three ways to dodge and burn; you get to determine which technique to use on any particular image. This first technique ("Quick Tone Improvement") is fast and can do the job for most images. The second technique ("Two-Layer Toning") balances speed with control. The last technique ("Smart Dodging and Burning") provides extreme control for highlights and shadows because of the prowess of Camera Raw.

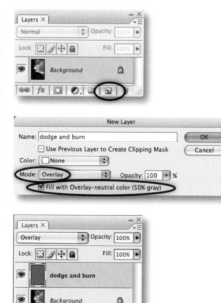

2. Add a Layer with a Blending Mode

To create a new layer above the original, press Option/Alt as you click the Create a New Layer icon in the Layers palette. Photoshop opens the New Layer dialog box. Name the layer and choose Overlay from the Mode menu.

Some blending modes lighten, some darken. The ones in the section headed by Overlay are the contrast blend modes, which can both lighten and darken the same layer. Any tone darker than 50% gray on the layer will darken (or *burn*) the layers below; any tone lighter than 50% on the layer will lighten (or *dodge*) the layers below; any tone at exactly 50% will be neutral, or invisible. Overlay is a good place to start. Soft Light is more subtle; you can change to Soft Light later to see how it affects your image. Select Fill With Overlay-Neutral Color (50% Gray), and click OK.

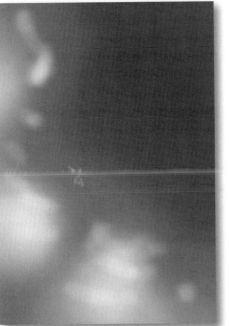

3. Paint a Mask

Photoshop just created a 50% gray layer. Because the blending mode regards 50% gray as being neutral, the layer currently has no effect. The trick is to minimally change the 50% tone to slightly lighter or darker to allow the layer to affect what's below. Choose the Brush tool and set up a good old-fashioned soft paintbrush (set the hardness to 0), leave it in Normal mode, and set the Opacity to somewhere between 5 and 15%. Set the foreground color to black and the background color to white to start. Paint over the light areas, such as the sky in this image, to bring out detail. You can paint over an area multiple times to keep darkening it, and you'll never corrupt your original image, because you're painting on a different layer. If there are subtle shades, they'll darken in a subtle manner.

When you want to paint over dark areas to lighten them, press X on the keyboard to exchange the foreground and background colors. Paint with white to lighten and with black to darken. In this image, painting white with a smaller brush over the human figure really brings out the detail.

Keep painting, moving from black to white (tapping X on your keyboard will allow you to toggle back and forth between the two) as appropriate to darken or lighten areas in the image. Nothing you do here can damage your original, so see how much detail you can pull out with a simple paintbrush.

To try a different blending mode, just select the "dodge and burn" layer in the Layers palette and choose a blending mode from the pop-up menu. Remember that Soft Light and Overlay behave the same way (they increase both saturation and contrast as you paint), but Overlay is more dramatic than Soft Light. ▥

T I P

Changing Colors. To quickly reset your foreground and background colors to the default black and white, respectively, press D on the keyboard or click the tiny icon **A** near the colors in the Tools palette.

To swap background and foreground colors, press X or click the double-arrow icon **B** in the Tools palette.

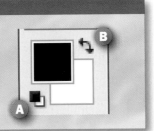

Two-Layer Toning

For a little more control when you dodge and burn, use two Adjustment Layers with different blending modes.

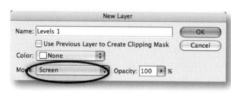

1. Add an Adjustment Layer

This technique uses blending modes, just as the last one did, but this time you'll use different blending modes for lightening and darkening the image. The sneaky bit here is that you'll use an Adjustment Layer that serves no purpose except as a vehicle for the blending mode.

Option/Alt-click the Create New Adjustment Layer icon in the Layers palette **A**. Choose Levels from the pop-up menu. (You can use any type of Adjustment Layer, really; you only want it for its blending mode and mask.) In the New Layer dialog box, name the Adjustment Layer and choose Screen from the Mode menu. The Screen blending mode halves the value of anything beneath it, essentially brightening the image by a factor of 2. Click OK to close the New Layer dialog box, and then click OK to close the Levels dialog box (that's right, without making an adjustment!) You'll let the blending mode do the heavy lifting.

2. Mask the Light Areas

Every Adjustment Layer comes with its own ready-to-go layer mask. Use a paintbrush with the foreground color set to black, and paint over the areas that are too light after the blending mode was applied. As you paint, more of the highlight detail returns. For example, in this image, paint over portions of the sky to bring back the detail in the clouds. You can also paint over the cliffs to exaggerate the play of light on the rocks, letting the original dark version of the image come through. Raise the Opacity of the brush when you want to bring in more detail. With a big soft brush, you don't have to worry too much about edge detail.

3. Add Another Adjustment Layer

To add density and pull out a little more information, use the same technique with a darkening blending mode. Start by adding another Adjustment Layer: press Option/Alt as you click the Create New Adjustment Layer icon, and choose Levels. This time, choose Multiply from the Mode menu. Multiply is the opposite of Screen. It doubles the values, creating a very dramatic change as everything is twice as dark as before. Click OK to close the New Layer dialog box and then click OK again to close the Levels dialog box.

4. Mask the Dark Areas

Paint with black wherever the image is too dark. The effect of the blending mode is reduced where you paint, and the underlying image shows through. You can even reduce the Opacity of the brush and paint over lighter areas such as the sky. (If you are only lightening or darkening small targeted areas, consider filling the layer masks with black and painting with white to reveal the adjustments, rather than painting with black and hiding areas you don't want the adjustments to be seen.)

©JHDAVIS

Making Separate "Exposures" from One Shot

Edit multiple versions of the same photo using Camera Raw, Smart Objects, and masks to precisely lighten and darken areas of an image.

1. Create Two Independent Smart Objects from the Image

For this technique, you need to have the same image appear twice, as two separate, independent Smart Objects in Photoshop. To do this we'll use a free script from Russell Brown called Dr. Brown's Services.

▶ *A link to the current version can be found at adventuresinphotoshop.com.*

This script provides a very easy way to create the two Smart Objects: Select the image in Bridge, and choose Tools > Dr. Brown's Services > Dr. Brown's Place-A-Matic 8 Bit. And that's all there is to it. Dr. Brown's Place-A-Matic opens any single file twice in Photoshop, retaining all the information associated with the original file, including a link to Camera Raw. Because the tonal correction will be done in Camera Raw, which always uses the highest bit-depth for its processing, there's no need to use 16-bit in Photoshop; 8-bit is fine.

2. Edit the First Smart Object to Gain Shadow Detail

Double-click the top Smart Object in the Layers palette to open it in Camera Raw. When you're editing this object, you're only concerned with the shadows; don't worry about losing information in the highlights. Increase Brightness, Fill Light, Contrast, and even Vibrance. You can also adjust Clarity, which creates targeted edge contrast, especially if you're working on a landscape. Move the slider until you begin to see halo artifacts, and then ease it back down a notch.

Note the *Clarity* and *Vibrance* settings so you can match those when you're working with highlights in the other object. Click OK to return to Photoshop.

3. Mask to Hide Excess

Of course, with the top Smart Object visible, the highlights are blown out. Click the Add A Mask icon in the Layers palette, then with a soft paintbrush, paint with black over the areas where you want to bring back the highlight detail. Wherever you paint, the top Smart Object is hidden, revealing the layer below, which has highlight detail.

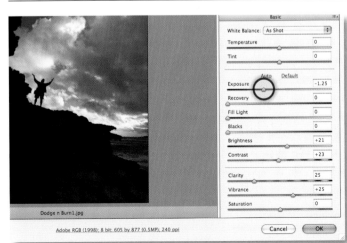

4. Edit the Second Smart Object to Pull Out Highlight Detail

Double-click the second Smart Object to open it in Camera Raw. Here, you care only about highlights; the shadow detail is safely in the top layer. Move Exposure to the right. You can also increase Brightness and Contrast. Match Clarity and Vibrance with the settings you used for the first layer. Click OK to return to Photoshop.

There's no need to add a mask to the bottom layer. The masking is being done in the top layer. ▥

©MARK BOROSCH PHOTOGRAPHY

Combining Bracketed Exposures

Quickly take the best detail from three different exposures to create one perfect image.

A

B

C

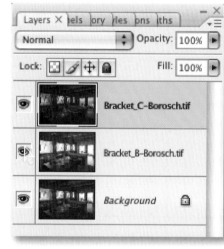

INSIGHT

Bracketing Exposures. Remember that the aperture, or the f-stop, in the camera affects not only how much light comes in but how much of the scene is in focus. That is, it controls the depth of field.

If you're using a point-and-click camera, point at different portions of the scene to lock in exposures.

1. Shoot Multiple Exposures

The human eye can change exposure on the fly, adjusting the size of the iris and the brain's reaction to light instantly. A camera is not nearly as responsive. It has a limited Dynamic Range (the tones from the lightest lights to the darkest darks where you want to see detail) that it can capture in a single shot. So when a scene contains more dynamic range than just one image can record, you can capture three different exposures—underexposed **A**, overexposed **B**, and middle exposure **C**—and combine them in Photoshop using layer masks and the amazing, though often misunderstood, Blend If sliders.

Many cameras can bracket automatically to provide you with three or more shots for a single scene. If your camera has a priority setting, set it to aperture priority so that it will be consistent for each exposure. If your camera doesn't have an aperture priority option, set it to landscape mode for best results. I usually bracket a full f/stop, which gives plenty of latitude to catch the dynamic range in the scenes.

If at all possible, use a tripod to keep the camera steady while you shoot.

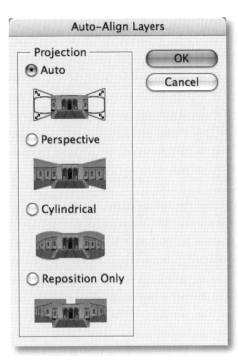

2. Align the Images in Photoshop

Open the images in Photoshop; the photographs for this project were taken by renowned photographer Mark Borosch. By default, they open as separate files. Select the layer in the Layers palette for one of the images and Shift-drag it onto the image window for the other image. Do the same for the third image, so that they're separate layers in a single file. For a shortcut, refer to the tip at left.

Even with an expensive tripod, there can be a slight discrepancy in the alignment of the exposures, and if they're even half-a-pixel off, you can get some nasty artifacts. To make sure the images are perfectly aligned (especially if you cheated and shot *without* a tripod), make sure all the layers are visible, Shift-click in the Layers palette to select them, and then choose Edit > Auto-Align Layers. In the Auto-Align Layers dialog box, select Auto, then click OK. Photoshop will rotate, scale, change perspective, and even perform a cylindrical warp if necessary to match the images.

3. Apply a Layer Mask

Our old friend the layer mask lets you bring in the detail from one exposure to another. Arrange the layers so that the darker, underexposed shot is at the top; the lighter, overexposed shot is in the middle; and the middle exposure is at the bottom. Select the middle layer.

For this step it's easier to hide everything on a layer and reveal only the detail you want from the image below. Start with a black layer mask. Option/Alt-click the Add a Layer Mask icon in the Layers palette; the entire mask is black. Set the foreground color to white. Use a big soft brush with opacity around 70% to paint in the parts of the image that have the detail you want. Change the brush size and Opacity to get different amounts of detail in different areas of the image.

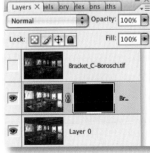

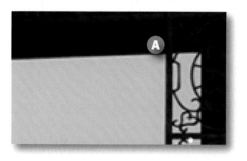

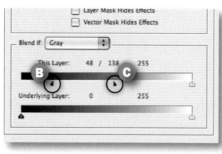

4. Adjust the Blend If Sliders

Where dark and light areas intermingle, as in the filigree in this image **A**, you could spend all day hand-painting a mask. But there's no reason to do that when Photoshop can do the work for you. *Select the top layer,* click the Layer Styles icon (*fx*) in the Layers palette, and choose Blending Options. Go directly to the Blend If sliders **B**, which may just become your new best friend.

The Blend If sliders let you control the visibility for the selected layer, as well as the underlying layers based upon the tones in the layers. For this procedure, you only need to worry about the *This Layer* slider, though. You can change what's visible and what's not visible based simply on the luminosity of the layer. Start by dragging the Black sliders on the left to the right and watch the underexposed shadow areas disappear, leaving only the highlights. Currently, when you move the slider, it decides whether each pixel is visible or not, with *no smooth transitions,* and the result can be very undesirable. The trick to getting good results is to *split* the slider.

To use the Blend If slider, then, with your darker exposure on top of the lighter one, drag the dark slider back to the left until you see the shadow detail you want, and then press Option/Alt and drag the right side of the slider until you see a nice transition between what's visible and what's hidden **C**. Everything to the *left* of the first dark triangle is *hidden*—there's a smooth transition to the next dark triangle—and everything to the *right* of this next triangle is visible.

You've quickly created a complex mask, and it's completely nondestructive. You can adjust the sliders at any time. 🎞

INSIGHT

High Dynamic Range (HDR). Photoshop CS2 introduced a feature called Merge to HDR (High Dynamic Range imagery), a great concept, but the technology wasn't really intended for photography as much as for video and 3D compositing. The results of combining multiple exposures using Merge to HDR *does* maintain the incredible number of colors and tones of all the exposures, but the problem with the Merge to HDR feature, including the upgraded version in CS3, is that the resulting image is usually… flat. While it is depicting a *true* "story" of the tonal range, it is not a *dynamic* story. I prefer a richer, hand-crafted story, so I combined the exposures manually in order to better convey the personality of the scene.

TIP

Fine-Tuning Visibility. To further fine-tune what's visible on a layer where you have used the Blend If options, there's nothing stopping you from adding a regular layer mask and painting out with black any excessive detail. Combining **automated** visibility of a layer with **Blend If** and manual visibility using good ol' **layer masks** gives you the best of both worlds!

Combining Background and Foreground Exposures

Quickly take the best detail from two different snapshots at different exposures to create one perfect image.

1. Capture the Moment, then Detail

This is an effective technique to use when the foreground and background require very different exposures, or if you find you have captured your subject with the correct exposure, but then after the moment passes, you would like to shoot and combine another shot that holds challenging background detail. Here, one image captures the women embracing in front of the Vietnam Memorial (the "moment"), and the other focuses on capturing the detail in the brightly lit trees and park in the background.

Transform

Auto-Align Layers...

Auto-Blend Layers

2. Align the Shots.

Bring both pictures into one Photoshop file and select the two layers by Shift-clicking on them in the Layers palette. Next, select Edit > Auto Align, then Auto.

3. Paint in the Detail

With the top (darker) layer active, Option/Alt-click on the Add A Mask icon. This creates a black-filled layer mask by default, thus allowing you to paint in the highlight detail where you want it by simply painting on the mask with a big, soft-edged, white-filled brush set to a low (20–50%) opacity. ▥

*Where the spirit does not
work with the hand,
there is no art.*

—LEONARDO DA VINCI

II

RETOUCHING & REPAIRING

©JHDAVIS

CHAPTER 6
Retouching Begins in Camera Raw

©JHDAVIS

THE PURPOSE OF RETOUCHING a photograph is to remove distractions that draw the eye and mind away from the subject and the story (whether cognitive, subliminal, or emotional) you are trying to tell.

Identifying exactly what is a distraction and what is an integral part of the personality of the person, place, or thing you photographed is one of those religious questions for tribal sages and advertising executives! Suffice it to say, as with most work in Photoshop CS3, it all begins in Adobe Camera Raw.

Foundational White Balance, Tone, and Vibrance Fixing

The first step to retouching an image is to set the basic color and tone that brings it to life.

©BROOKE CHRISTL PHOTOGRAPHY

1. Open the Image in Camera Raw

In Bridge, select the images you want to work with. Press Shift to select contiguous images or Command/Ctrl to select images that aren't next to each other. Then, to open the images in Camera Raw without also opening Photoshop, choose File > Open In Camera Raw (or press Command/Ctrl-R).

2. Set the White Balance

Typically, the first step is to adjust the white balance. Select the White Balance tool in the upper left of the toolbar and click an area of the image that should be a neutral color: dark, light, or middle gray. Experiment by clicking on different areas—all these changes are nondestructive.

Another approach is to choose Auto from the White Balance menu in the Basic panel. Fine-tune the color with the Tint and Temperature sliders.

Depending on what you want to convey, a warmer color cast may be desirable. Here, the veil's cool tones accentuate the warmer face.

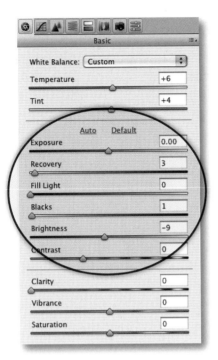

3. Adjust the Tone

In the middle of the Basic panel, click Auto to let Camera Raw take a stab at adjusting the tone. Auto often brightens the midtones too much, but it usually sets nice white and black points. Adjust the Exposure setting if necessary; press Option/Alt as you drag the slider to see where clipping is taking place. After adjusting Exposure, verify that the Blacks slider is in the right place. The Blacks slider sets the black point in the image; again, you can press Option/Alt to see where clipping is occurring.

Now, adjust the Brightness slider. In most cases, you'll want to decrease the brightness. You can also move the Fill Light slider to pull in more detail in the shadows. The Recovery slider brings out highlight details, but if the Exposure is set correctly, it can be left quite low.

For a portrait, be careful with the Contrast slider and the Clarity slider. Clarity provides localized edge contrast, not what you typically want for this type of photo.

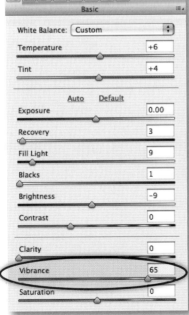

4. Add Vibrance

Increase the Vibrance to give a wonderful punch to color in the hair, eyes, and even the background of a portrait. Vibrance increases saturation in a non-linear way. It boosts the areas that are undersaturated. And Vibrance is ideal for a portrait, because it's conservative with the orange-browns that underlie most skin tones.

Vibrance is a great alternative to Saturation, which increases saturation uniformly, and can result in a sun-burned look.

We also added our mandatory Vignette from over in the Lens Corrections panel. See Insight on page 89 for more on vignetting. ▥

Removing Dust and Healing Blemishes

If there are numerous areas to heal or retouch in your photos, you'll work more quickly and with more flexibility using Photoshop's Healing and Cloning tools. But the Retouch tool in Camera Raw can be a real timesaver if you need to repair just a few distracting glitches or spots created by a dusty camera sensor or lens.

Healing with the Retouch Tool

The Retouch tool has two modes: Clone and Heal. Clone replaces the selected area with an exact copy of the source area. Heal blends the repaired area into the surrounding pixels. Nine times out of ten, you'll get the best results using Heal mode.

To use the Retouch tool, click the center of the area you want to heal, and drag the cursor to cover the anomaly. The Retouch tool finds its own source area to use to replace the area you've covered, but you can drag the source to a different spot if you need to.

If the anomalies are all a similar size, you don't need to drag over each one. Just click on each anomaly, and then verify that the Retouch tool selected an appropriate source.

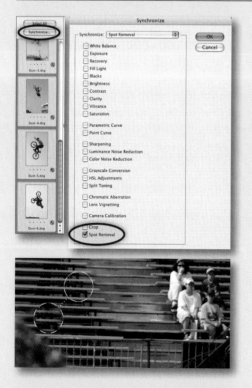

Removing Lens Dust Spots

If the camera sensor or lens had spots on it when the photo was shot, those dust spots show up on the image. And typically they'll be in the same location for every image taken during the same photo shoot.

To quickly correct the problem for all the images from the shoot, *first heal the dust spots in one image.* Next, select that image in the Filmstrip, and then select the other images you want to fix. Click **Synchronize**. In the Synchronize dialog box, select **Spot Removal.** Camera Raw applies the same healing to each of the other images in the shoot. Check each image to make sure that the selected source area is appropriate for each healed area, as what's happening there changes from image to image. If a dust spot is already hidden by texture in the photo, you can click on and delete that correction (like we'll do in the bleachers shot to the left).

If you know there is a lot of dust on your lens, take a reference shot against a wall or sky out of focus before you shoot the photos. That way you'll have one shot that clearly shows you where all the dust spots are located.

If you can't easily locate all the dust spots, exaggerate the contrast, clarity, and possibly the brightness of the image so you can see them. Then, after you've removed the dust spots, don't forget to return to the original settings! ▦

Color Enhancements

The last correction stop for most images in Camera Raw is the HSL/Grayscale panel. There, you can punch up the vividness of specific colors or sculpt the world's best black-and-white conversion.

For a special touch on your grayscale images, turn to Camera Raw's Split-Toning panel.

Targeting Saturation and Luminance

©BROOKE CHRISTL PHOTOGRAPHY

Camera Raw is all about global editing, but even so, you can target specific areas based on hue. Using the HSL/Grayscale panel, you can optimize skin, hair, and even eyes without so much as a mask.

Also, if individual hues are off, you can shift them in the HSL/Grayscale panel. In this image, however, the colors are all set, so you can move directly to the Saturation tab.

By increasing the yellows in the **Saturation** tab, you can intensify the hair color. It's that easy. As you make changes in this panel, remember to move neighboring colors in the same direction as well, so that the transition from one adjusted color to its neighbor is smooth.

Adjust sliders on the Luminance tab to lighten up skin tone or smooth out the overall look. For example, move the Oranges slider to lighten or darken the skin tone, and then move the Reds and Yellows sliders slightly, too, to even out the transition.

Black & White and More

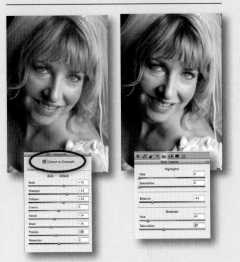

To change a color image to black-and-white, click **Convert To Grayscale**. The Hue, Saturation, and Luminance tabs are replaced with the single Grayscale Mix tab. The sliders on this tab give you a great deal of control, much better than in even the newest black-and-white adjustment features in Photoshop.

Click **Auto** to see what it suggests. Notice the curve formed by the slider handles, creating smooth transitions. Accept the suggestions as a starting point and tweak them as you like. Or, click **Default** to zero out the sliders, and then move them yourself.

Use the Split Toning panel to add subtle color richness to a grayscale image. Add one color throughout the tonal range, or different colors for highlights and shadows. Of course, just because you *can* add yellow to shadows and purple to highlights doesn't mean that you *should*. I prefer to increase the saturation of the shadows, specify a color for them, and use the Balance slider to determine where the color appears. I leave the Highlights sliders alone, because adding color to the highlights often makes the image muddier.

©BROOKE CHRISTL PHOTOGRAPHY

Sharpening Portraits

Camera Raw gives you the creative control you need when sharpening portraits to bring out the detail without exaggerating flaws.

TIP

See Detail Clearly. To minimize distractions from color and see the actual luminosity sharpening that's being performed, preview the sharpening in grayscale: Press Option/Alt as you move the Amount slider.

Detail

Sharpening

Amount	0
Radius	1.0
Detail	25
Masking	0

Noise Reduction

Luminance	0
Color	0

Zoom preview to 100% or larger to see the effects of the controls in this panel.

---

1. Open the Detail Panel

Camera Raw is the place to perform your initial global sharpening. Remember that you can always further sharpen targeted areas, such as the eyes, in Photoshop. In Camera Raw, the goal is to emphasize the areas of significance without sharpening the subtleties, such as the skin.

Select the Detail panel to get started. Then, zoom in to 100% or greater so you can preview the sharpening effects.

A shortcut for zooming to 100% is double-clicking on the Magnifying Glass Zoom tool or Command/Option-0 or Ctrl/Alt-0. The associated shortcut for Fit in Window is double-clicking on the Hand tool, or Command/Ctrl-0.

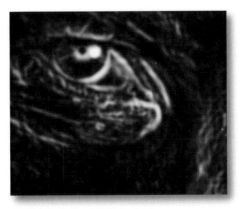

▶ **See adventuresinphotoshop.com for more on recommended plug-ins.**

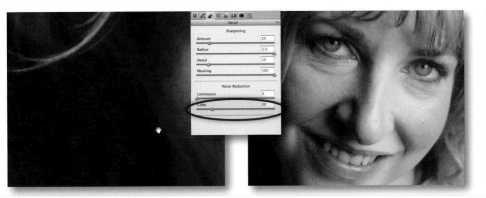

Sharpen with Presets. The How to Wow presets includes a series of sharpening presets, some designed for landscapes, others for portraiture. The landscape presets sharpen every pixel, with higher Amount, subpixel Radius, and lower Masking values. Portrait presets are more forgiving for skin tone, and use lower Amount, higher Radius, and higher Masking values. Use a preset as a starting point, and then tweak the settings for your image.

2. Adjust the Sliders

The Amount slider determines the intensity of the sharpening. Move it a little to the right, but keep it low for base sharpening on an image. If you were preparing a final image for printing (in other words, you didn't plan to open the file in Photoshop and do final sharpening there), you could use a more aggressive Amount.

Next, set your Radius based upon the inherent sharpness of your original. If the file is already in sharp focus, you can use a lower setting (often below 1 pixel) to minimize the chance of edge artifacts. If your original is the slightest bit out of focus, use a higher radius to include all the portions of the softer edges.

Detail sets the intensity of the sharpening within the Radius. Be conservative with this slider, especially when you're working with portraits. Keep it as low as possible, because artifacts appear at higher values. That said, it's okay if some of the wrinkles and skin anomalies are sharpened, because you'll take care of that with the Masking slider.

The Masking slider is almost magical. It restricts sharpening to edge detail. With Masking high, you can sharpen the eyes without emphasizing skin anomalies. Press Option/Alt as you move the slider to see where sharpening is occurring. For a portrait, you can set masking between 50 and 100 without a problem.

3. Reduce Noise

If there is color noise in your portrait, move the Color slider to the right. A little color noise reduction goes a long way. Even at 10, the color is blurred and blended back into the file. Luminance noise reduction is much less effective, unfortunately, and can result in a watercolor effect. You're usually better off without it. I've had much better luck in Photoshop with the Noiseware Pro plug-in from Imagenomic. ▦

CHAPTER 7
Smart Skin-Softening and Color Unifying

©JHDAVIS

S KIN. Whether smooth, ruddy, freckly, pale, dark, or pimply, we seem to have an infatuation with it, especially the skin on our faces! It serves as a canvas of sorts for portraits, and we notice it immediately.

If only we could truly soften skin with a command and balance our color variations with a slider! While that's not physically possible (at least not yet), why not take advantage of the next best thing: Photoshop. When images of ourselves or family or our clients end up in print of some sort for all posterity, we might as well take advantage of Photoshop's skin power tools to remove distracting details and allow the personality of the subject to shine through.

Softening Skin

Nondestructive Smart Filters are all you need to soften skin anomalies, including large pores, makeup dust, and five o'clock shadow.

1. Open as a Smart Object

After you've made your global changes in Camera Raw, click Open Object. *Note:* If Open Image is the option in the lower-right of Camera Raw's interface, hold down the Shift key and it will toggle to Open Object **A**.

The image opens as a Smart Object layer in Photoshop. Because it's a Smart Object, it remembers everything that you've done to it in Camera Raw, so you can return there to change settings at any time. Smart Objects also let you apply Smart Filters, which perform the same tasks as filters without making the changes permanent.

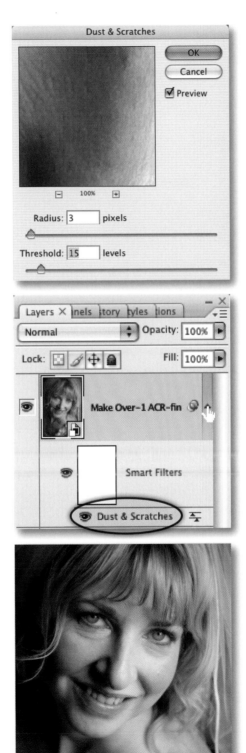

2. Apply the Dust & Scratches Filter

Many filters can be used for softening skin, but in this project we'll use one of my favorites. Start by choosing Filter > Noise > Dust & Scratches. As its name suggests, this filter is effective for removing dust and scratches from antique or battered photographs. But here it's useful for removing skin anomalies such as distracting pores or five o'clock shadow.

First, move the Radius up to get rid of the artifacts: Zoom in to an area in your image where the change will be obvious, such as the texture on the nose in this portrait. Move the Radius up one pixel at a time until the artifacts are gone.

At this point, everything is being softened, including the basic noise structure of the photograph. Be careful not to "smoosh" that structure. A sure sign of a bad retouching job is that some portions of the image have a texture or noise and others are buttery smooth. To reduce the softening in areas that don't warrant it, move the Threshold slider up until you can see the basic structure of the skin and the noise of the file—but not so high that you reintroduce the anomalies you wanted to remove. The Threshold slider determines when the filter kicks in. For this image, anomalies reappear at a threshold of 35, but at 15 they're gone. Notice that much of the detail in the eyes and other areas of contrast return when you increase the Threshold. Subtleties are softened, but areas that aren't so subtle aren't affected.

Click OK to close the filter dialog box. The Dust & Scratches filter appears in the Layers palette, along with an empty filter mask. Smart Filters are nondestructive, so what's recorded here is the *process* of applying the filter. Pixels haven't been altered, so you can always go back and edit the filter settings later (and the filter's Opacity and Blend Mode as well).

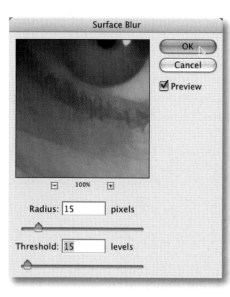

3. Apply the Surface Blur Filter

The Dust & Scratches filter removed anomalies, but it didn't soften the skin overall. This is where the Surface Blur filter comes in. Choose Filter > Blur > Surface Blur.

In the Surface Blur dialog box, the Radius setting determines how much blurring occurs, and the Threshold setting determines when it kicks in. However, the Threshold setting works differently from the one in the Dust & Scratches filter. No blurring takes place when the Threshold slider is at the far left; as you move it to the right, more blurring occurs.

Increase the Radius, and then increase the Threshold. This image looks good when both sliders are set at 15. The settings to use depend on your image, its resolution, and the amount of softening you want to do. There's still a slightly artificial, watercolor look, but the next step will take care of that.

INSIGHT

Using Surface Blur Elsewhere. The Surface Blur filter is a great tool for blurring the background of an image to shorten the apparent depth-of-field. Move the Threshold slider to the far right to do so.

▶ See page 50 for more on this technique.

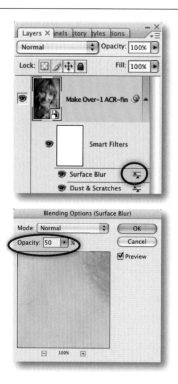

4. Adjust the Filter's Opacity

To pull some detail back into the image, reduce the intensity of the filter by reducing its Opacity. Double-click the icon to the right of the Surface Blur filter name. Then adjust the Opacity to about 50%. That brings 50% of the detail back throughout the file. Every pore and eyelash is there, but the image has been softened.

5. Mask the Areas You Don't Want to Soften

Of course, the goal was to soften the skin, not the entire image. The filter mask that automatically comes along with Smart Filters lets you control where the softening takes place. Select the filter mask in the Layers palette. Make sure black is the foreground color, select a soft brush, and set the opacity of the brush to about 50%. You'll paint back in the detail by punching a hole in the mask, allowing the original sharp image to show through.

First, brush the eyes, eyelashes, and eyebrows, so that the eye detail returns but the area under the eye remains softened. The eyes are certainly the most important part of a portrait.

Then, paint any other areas that require more detail. In the image of the bride, paint in some detail around the hair, the edge of the wedding gown, and the mouth. Sharpen the areas that will clearly indicate that the image is in focus, such as specular highlights.

To see the mask itself, Option/Alt-click on its thumbnail; you can then see the mask as you paint to clean it up. ▥

Unifying Skin Color and Tone

Target color adjustments to even the skin tone in an image where the subject suffers from rosacea, sunburn, or an overly enthusiastic application of rouge.

©BROOKE CHRISTL PHOTOGRAPHY

Set the Sample Size. The eyedroppers throughout Photoshop's dialog boxes collect samples based on the settings for the Eyedropper tool. So, before you add a Hue/Saturation Adjustment Layer, make sure the sample size is appropriate. Select the Eyedropper tool, and then choose 5 x 5 from the Sample Size menu in the Options bar. A point sample selects only a single pixel—not good for skin tone. 5 x 5 Average provides a more representative sampling. Use larger sampling areas to remove a color cast. For instance, for fixing white balance with the Levels or Curves gray eyedropper, try a setting of 11 x 11 or higher.

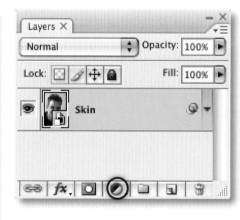

HTW See page 27 to learn how to locate this book's follow-along images, cinematic tutorials, downloadable freebies, and useful links!

1. Add a Hue/Saturation Adjustment Layer

The Hue/Saturation dialog box has everything you need to perform a very targeted color adjustment with more control than you can achieve in Camera Raw.

Open the image in Photoshop. Then, click the Create New Adjustment Layer icon in the Layers palette, and choose Hue/Saturation. You'll use the Hue/Saturation Adjustment Layer to make both targeted and global adjustments. Though the focus of this lesson is on unifying skin tones, you'd use the same technique to shift any specific color without affecting other colors in a photograph— from a car to a dress to a gadget.

Adjustment Layers are nondestructive, even when you're not working with a Smart Object. You can always undo or fine-tune the Adjustment Layer settings later.

2. Select a Basic Color Group

By default, the Hue/Saturation dialog box makes global color changes. The sampling eyedroppers aren't even available when Master is selected from the menu at the top. So, the first step for targeted color changes is to select a color group. Choose the color closest to the one you want to change (Reds, in this case), but it doesn't need to be perfect. This is merely a starting point.

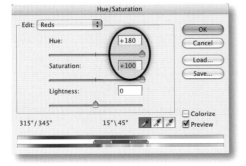

3. Exaggerate Hue and Saturation

Depending on the subtlety of the changes you're making, you may not be able to see them easily. To see more clearly which areas you are trying to adjust, first exaggerate the Hue and Saturation settings. Shift the Hue slider to 180 degrees and push the Saturation slider to 100. Certainly, the skin tone becomes less than attractive, but you can definitely identify the areas that are being adjusted.

4. Move the Sliders Together

The sliders at the bottom of the dialog box show how colors are affected. The top bar shows the original color and the bottom bar shows the color it's been mapped to. In this example, what was red is now cyan. Colors outside of the targeted range—blues, yellows, and greens—are unaffected.

Move the sliders together to isolate a very specific portion of the color range. It doesn't have to be the perfect area—anything close to the area you want to change will do.

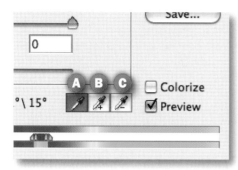

5. Sample Specific Target Colors

Select the eyedropper **A**, and then click on the image to sample a specific color you want to adjust. You may need to zoom in to find the areas you most want to modify. If it's helpful, temporarily deselect the Preview option to see the original image without the colorful distractions.

Select all the colors you want to manipulate: To add colors to the selection, press Shift as you click within the image, or select the Add To Sample eyedropper **B**. To remove colors from the selection, Option/Alt-click or select the Subtract From Sample eyedropper **C**.

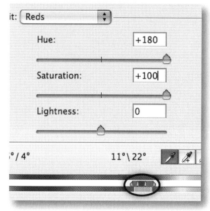

6. Drag the Triangle Sliders to Create a Transition

The sliders at the bottom of the dialog box have moved to reflect the colors you've selected. The colors between the two vertical bars shift completely. The areas between the vertical bars and the triangle sliders are adjusted partially. Anything outside the triangle bars is completely unaffected.

To create a smooth transition, then, drag the triangle sliders farther from the vertical bars.

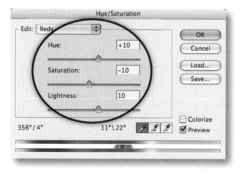

7. Adjust the Hue, Saturation, and Lightness Sliders

So far, everything you've done has been to *select* the colors you want to adjust. Now, make the actual adjustments. First, move the Hue and Saturation sliders back down to 0. Then, fine-tune the Hue, Saturation, and Lightness sliders. As you make the adjustment, you may discover that you missed a set of colors; you can still add them using the Add To Sample eyedropper. For this portrait we moved the Hue of the selected red blotches toward the yellows and desaturated and lightened the blotches as well.

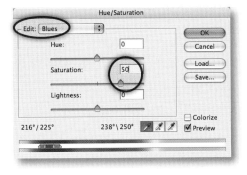

8. Make Targeted Adjustments for Other Areas

You can use the same technique to adjust other colors as well. Repeat steps 2–7 to heighten the blues in the eyes, for example. The same steps apply whether you're working with reds, yellows, blues, or a different set of colors: Select a color group, exaggerate hue and saturation, move the range sliders together, sample the target colors, create a transition, and make the actual adjustments.

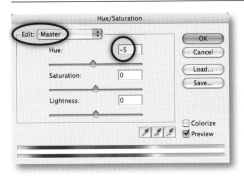

9. Make Global Adjustments

After you've made targeted color adjustments, evaluate whether the overall color needs to be shifted. In this example, the overall tone had become just a little too yellow. To make a global adjustment, choose Master from the menu, and then shift the sliders for the effect you want.

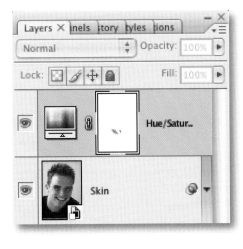

10. Mask Areas to Return Original Color

There is some overlap in colors in different areas of the image, so even though you're targeting specific colors, you may affect areas you wanted to leave unchanged. For example, reducing the reds in the skin tone also reduces the red in the lips. Use the layer mask that comes with an Adjustment Layer to bring back color from the original image.

Paint in black on the mask where you want to hide the effects of the Adjustment Layer and reveal the original image. To return color to the lips, for example, paint over them with a soft, low-opacity brush. ▥

CHAPTER 8
Portrait Patching and Wrinkle Reduction

AT WHAT POINT do creases in the skin go from "smile lines" to "crow's feet," from being a part of the character of a person to becoming a distraction from that same character? Well, as the saying goes, "Photoshop doesn't create plastic people, **people** create plastic people."

In this chapter we'll give you a few of our favorite techniques for minimizing "distractions" in a portrait. What you consider a distraction I'll leave between you, your priest, and your client!

©BROOKE CHRISTI PHOTOGRAPHY

Removing Shine

Add a little digital powder with a patch to reduce the shine on a forehead, nose, or other skin area.

1. Add an Empty Layer

Most of the changes you've made so far in this section, and in most of the book, have been procedural. Because you've been using Smart Objects, you could revisit your decisions, adjust settings, and even return to the original image. However, for more comprehensive retouching, you have to change some actual pixels. Even using pixel-changing tools, though, you can still sometimes protect yourself from permanent changes. And that's what you'll do here.

Click the Create New Layer icon in the Layers palette to add an empty layer above the existing layer. Name it Patch. Then zoom in to the problem area, so you can see it clearly.

2. Set Up the Healing Brush Tool

Select the Healing Brush tool (🖊). It modifies the area you paint based on the source sample you've selected. It then "heals" the area by automatically blending the edges with the surrounding pixels. Because the blending is built into the Healing Brush tool, you can get away with using a hard-edged brush. To remove the shine on the forehead, set the Hardness to 80–85%. Select as large a brush as you can for the area you need to cover.

Deselect Aligned in the Options bar. When that option is selected, the Healing Brush tool samples pixels continuously. Deselect it so that you can use the same sample area over and over again.

3. Select a Source Sample

The Healing Brush uses the texture of the source area, but not necessarily the color or the tone, so you may be able to retouch a large area without needing to resample. Choose All Layers (or Current and Below, if you have adjustment layers visible above your patch layer) from the Sample menu in the Options bar; the tool will sample the content on every layer in the file at the point you click. It's that ability that makes it possible for you to retouch on an empty layer.

Option/Alt-click to create the source sample. If you'll be retouching a large area, sample from a similar large area so you won't have to resample as often.

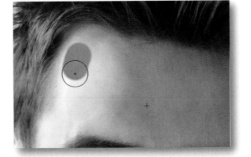

4. Heal the Offending Area

After you've set the source, use short strokes to cover the offending area. You can change the brush size as you work to accommodate narrower or wider areas. In this example, we're just painting over the area that's a little too shiny and distracting.

TIP

Undo Strategically. In general, you shouldn't be using the Undo command very often. Work with nondestructive features, such as Smart Filters and adjustment layers, to avoid the need to undo. But when you're working with the Healing Brush tool, the Undo command can be a good friend.

5. Heal Contrasting Edges

Be careful as you heal areas that abut contrasting content, such as hair or backgrounds. Remember that the Healing Brush tool will blend the area you paint with the pixels surrounding it, and that could get quite messy. Sample from an area that has similar contrast (like a neighboring hairline), and be prepared to undo anything that doesn't look quite right.

6. Apply a Blending Mode

The patch is okay, but it's almost certain to be a little heavy-handed. Since you're wanting to remove distractions, not introduce them, take advantage of a blending mode to reduce the effect.

Choose Darken (or Darker Color for a variation) from the Blending Mode menu in the Layers palette. When Darken is applied, pixels that are the same as or lighter than layers below will have no effect; only darker pixels on this layer will show. The blending mode could help the transition, especially around the hairline.

7. Reduce the Opacity

The blending mode helps, but changing the patch layer's Opacity can make a real difference. Remember, you are trying to minimize distracting highlights, not get rid of the natural lighting on the subject. Reduce the Opacity until the patch looks more realistic. If you've done a good job with the Healing Brush tool, the overall color should be fine. You just want to make sure you have a smooth transition between the patch and the rest of the skin. For this example, 45–50% Opacity works pretty well.

Patching Skin

Minimize awkward shadows or remove larger distractions using the Healing Brush.

1. Set Up the Healing Brush

First, create a new empty layer named Patch. Then, select the Healing Brush tool. Select All Layers from the Sample menu so that you can sample from the layers below. Deselect Aligned and set the brush size and hardness. For an area slightly out of focus, try a softer brush.

TIP

Focus Is a Patch Challenge. In an out-of-focus image, you may not get great results because there may not be enough information in the samples for the tool to work effectively. However, you can compensate for irregularities by reducing the Opacity of the Patch layer.

2. Paint Over Shadowy Areas

Option/Alt-click to select a sample. Use short strokes to make sure you remain within the appropriate sample area. As you drag the brush, it uses the color, tone, and from the source area, but when you release the mouse, it picks up color and tone from the pixels around it. Remember to undo anything that really looks wrong, but don't panic if the result is a little heavier than you planned.

3. Reduce the Opacity

Remember that the goal is primarily to reduce the distraction caused by an unexpected shadow. Select the layer and then reduce the opacity in the Layers palette. In this example, 35% gives the even transition we want. 🔲

©BROOKE CHRISTL PHOTOGRAPHY

Patching Hair

Duplicate portions of the hair and transform them for a natural effect, whether you're emphasizing the shine or filling in a distracting "empty" spot.

1. Make a Selection

The Lasso tool (⟨⟩) comes in very handy when you want to select an irregular shape such as a lock of hair. Select the Lasso tool, and then enter 5 pixels in the Feather field in the Options bar to soften the edges of the selection.

2. Copy the Selection to a New Layer

If you've made your selection on the image layer, choose Layer > New > Layer Via Copy to copy it to its own layer. If, however, you made the selection on a layer other than the image layer, choose Edit > Copy Merged to copy everything that's visible under the selection, no matter what layer it's on. Then, choose Edit > Paste. Photoshop pastes the selection onto its own new layer. Name the new layer Patch Hair.

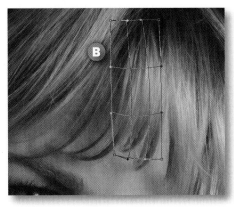

3. Transform the Selection

Choose Edit > Free Transform. Then, move the patch wherever you want it. You can rotate it and scale it so that it fits its new environment **A**. Using the Free Transform command to move a selected and copied area gives you much more control than the Patch tool.

To further change the patch so it looks even less like the source area, click the Warp Mode icon **B** in the Options bar. In Warp mode, a grid overlies the patch, and you can manipulate the grid to warp different portions of the selection.

Click the Commit button **C** in the Options bar or simply double-click to accept the changes you made.

4. Add and Adjust Copies

Duplicate the layer by choosing Layer > Duplicate Layer (or select a different area with the Lasso to use as a patch). Name the layer. Then, choose Edit > Free Transform, move the patch where you want it, and make Paste transformations. Create as many copies as you need to create the effect you want.

5. Blend in the Duplicates

To create a smoother transition, use the Eraser tool (🩹) to blend in the copies. Set the tool to be big and soft, with an opacity around 50%. Move the Eraser tool around the edges of the patches, anywhere they look unnatural. In this example, the goal is to have the hair shine more consistently across the forehead, and you don't really even notice the individual strands. The test is whether the results appear believable. Keep working on the transitions until they're smooth. 🎞

©BROOKE CHRISTL PHOTOGRAPHY

Reducing Wrinkles

Brush out distractions without sacrificing the personality of your subject.

1. Set Up the Healing Brush

Often, you want to reduce the effect of wrinkles, bags under the eyes, five o'clock shadow, or other skin attributes without removing them altogether. The Healing Brush is able to completely remove anomalies, but you can also use it to merely temper them. As always, start by creating a new layer for the retouching you'll do. Click the Create New Layer icon, and then name the layer Reduce.

Select the Healing Brush tool. Where the image is in sharp focus, you can use a fairly hard brush. Make sure Aligned is deselected, and choose All Layers from the Sample menu in the Options bar.

See page 27 to learn how to locate this book's follow-along images, cinematic tutorials, downloadable freebies, and useful links!

2. Heal Wrinkles and Other Anomalies

Option/Alt-click to select a sample source with matching skin texture. Then, brush over the areas under the eyes using short strokes to ensure you stay within the appropriate sample area. Where there's a mascara blotch or any other irregularity, approach it with caution. To heal areas that abut contrasting colors, resample a source that has a similar edge.

Paint over any other anomalies in the skin. The Healing Brush blends them into the surrounding area.

3. Use Opacity to Moderate Healing

Most photos won't look very natural if you remove wrinkles or shadows completely. To ease them back in, change the layer's Opacity. I think of this as dial-an-age, because you can reduce the wrinkles as much as you want to.

If one Opacity setting works well for most of the anomalies you healed, but not for others, choose the highest Opacity setting. You can use a layer mask to bring back the detail in other areas, as we'll do next.

4. Add a Layer Mask

To reduce the amount of healing in specific areas, use a layer mask. Click the Add A Layer Mask icon in the Layers palette to create a mask. Then, select the Brush tool and set its Opacity to about 50%. Make sure black is the current foreground color, and then paint wherever you want to bring back more of the original texture.

For the bride, I set the layer opacity to 70%, then painted the mask under her eyes to bring back some of the detail so viewers of the portrait wouldn't think plastic surgery had taken place.

CHAPTER 9
Reshaping Portraits and Body Parts

WE'RE TAKING OFF THE GLOVES and moving from the ring of retouching subtle distractions to the field of outright manipulation and misrepresentation!

Since I have ethical issues regarding much of the fashion industry's portrayal of women as needing to be both anorexic and prepubescent in order to be "Beautiful," I have chosen to use a more lighthearted subject matter to teach the very useful capabilities of Liquify and some techniques for creative body lighting. I hope you enjoy this "variation on a theme." (Note: I would put a smiley face here, but my editor won't let me.)

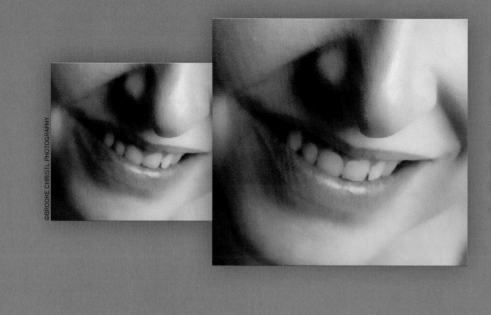

©BROOKE CHRISTL PHOTOGRAPHY

Selectively Reshaping Portraits

Gently redefine the lines of the lips, gums, and other facial features to minimize distractions in a portrait.

1. Isolate the Area of Interest

The Liquify filter makes short work of reshaping facial features, but it doesn't work with Smart Objects. To use the filter, you need to isolate the area you want to work with and move it to its own layer.

First, use the Lasso tool or the Marquee tool with no feathering to select the area you want to modify. Then, choose Edit > Copy Merged to copy all the content on every layer under your selection. It may take a moment for Photoshop to copy it all if there are several layers.

Next, choose Edit > Paste. Photoshop pastes the selection on its own layer. Name the layer Reshape.

Now, to reduce the area the filter has to calculate, load the layer as a selection: move the cursor over the layer thumbnail, and then press Command/Ctrl-click. Photoshop loads the selection. This method works anytime you want to select any portion of a layer that is surrounded by transparency.

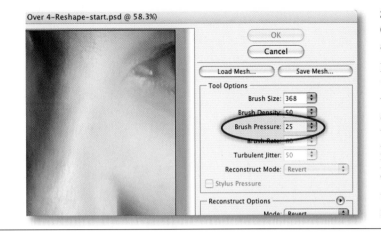

Over 4-Reshape-start.psd @ 58.3%

2. Apply the Liquify Filter

Choose Filter > Liquify. The filter will affect only the selected area.

By default, Brush Pressure is set to 100%. That would be perfect if you were creating comic book caricatures for a children's birthday party, but for most uses, that's far too much pressure. When you use the Liquify filter, lower the Brush Pressure to 25% as a new default. The Brush Pressure setting affects every tool in the filter, and 25% provides much more control.

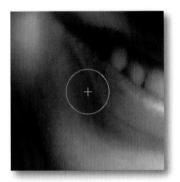

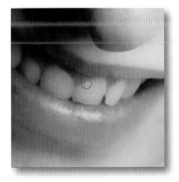

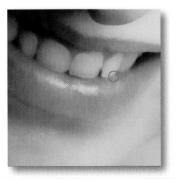

3. Reshape Using the Push Left Tool

Select the Push Left tool (). This tool should really be called the Shift Pixels tool, because which direction the pixels go depends on how you're moving the tool. The Push Left tool gives you a great deal of control, which is what you want when you're reshaping body parts.

Use the edge of the brush to paint along lip lines, gum lines, and other delicate features that could benefit from just a little gentle reshaping. As you stroke down, pixels move to the *right*; as you stroke up, they move to the *left*. To switch the direction and move pixels to the left as you paint downward, press Option/Alt as you brush. Use the edge of the brush, rather than the center, for more subtle changes. For super-sensitive areas, lower the brush pressure to 10.

For the best results, retouch each line in one fell swoop. If you hack away at the target area, you'll end up with a mess. Aim for one smooth curve, creating an organic shape. Feel free to undo and try again until you get the look you want. The exception to making the change in one fell swoop is when you want extreme subtlety, such as when reshaping a gum line; then you may want to use a very light brush pressure with multiple strokes.

4. Pucker to Alter the Specular Highlights

Unless you're working with images from a fashion shoot, you probably don't want to give your subject a noticeable rhinoplasty. However, you can make subtle changes that minimize distraction. For example, the way the light hits the bride's nose in this image emphasizes the end of the nose. Reshaping the specular highlight can take care of that.

Select the Pucker tool (🦟). This is a powerful tool, and one that demands respect—and caution. Use a brush that's bigger than the area you want to affect. Then click on the area once or twice, stopping after each click to see the effect. In this example, two quick clicks are all it takes to slightly reduce the nose, just enough to make it less distracting.

When you're satisfied with the changes you've made in the Liquify dialog box, click OK to close it and return to the full image. ▥

Reshaping Bodies

Help a friend (whether a drinking buddy or a super model) go from flabby to fit without all that pesky exercise. It's easy enough with the Liquify filter—and a few extra tricks.

1. Duplicate the Layer

When you're reshaping an entire body, rather than just the details, you can take advantage of several features in Photoshop. They all require actual pixel manipulation, though, so I recommend duplicating the *Background* layer right off the bat. That way you can always return to your original if things go awry.

Press Command/Option-J or Ctrl/Alt-J to duplicate and rename the layer at the same time; call it Skinnify.

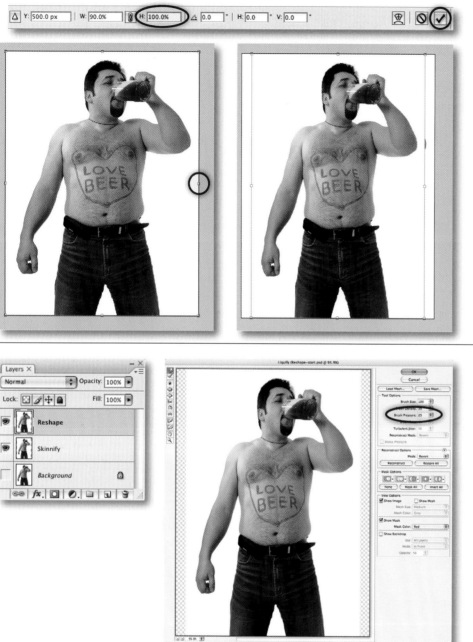

2. Instant 10% Weight Loss

This first step is so easy, it almost feels like cheating. If your portrait or figure shot is straight on, without dramatic perspective, you can slim the person with one quick step.

Choose Edit > Free Transform. Then press Option/Alt as you pull the side handles in to 90%, for a 10% reduction. Pressing Option/Alt lets you scale both sides from the center. Keep your eye on the horizontal scale box in the Options bar. Anything less than 90% is too greedy and won't look natural.

Click the Commit button or double-click in the transformation area. Your subject already looks skinnier. Hide the Background layer so that the original image isn't sticking out behind the new layer.

3. Apply the Liquify Filter

Before you go any further, duplicate and rename the Skinnify layer as you did the Background so you can get back to this stage easily.

Now you're ready to make the big changes, the kind that usually come about after months of diet and fitness regimens.

Choose Filter > Liquify to open the Liquify dialog box. Change the Brush Pressure to 25%, a good default for most of the tools in the filter.

Because there was no selection, the entire layer comes into the Liquify dialog box.

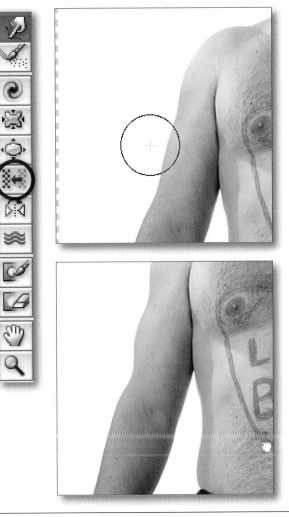

4. Define Muscle Contours with a Push

Zoom in to see the area you're working with. Select the Push Left tool (), which I think of as the Shift Pixels tool, and set up a fairly large brush. Paint with the edge of the brush, rather than the center of the brush. You can use the Push Left tool to manipulate the edges of the arms so that you plump up the muscles and remove a little extra flab.

When you brush down with the Push Left tool, it actually pushes pixels to the right. Drag the brush down the edge of the arm to give it a little more definition. Don't be shy about using the Undo command. You'll get the best results if you make the changes in one fell swoop, so that it looks organic. Keep undoing until you get the look you want.

Brushing upward pushes pixels to the left—or you can push pixels to the left by pressing Option/Alt as you brush downward. Reduce the brush pressure in some areas to keep the changes subtle.

Of course, there are two other directions pixels can go: Brush to the right to move pixels up. Brush to the left to move them down.

5. Protect Specific Areas

If you're working in tight quarters, you could accidentally shift pixels in an area you didn't want to change. To *protect* an area, select the Freeze Mask tool (). The Liquify filter uses liquid as an analogy, so it makes sense that freezing an area would keep it from flowing. For the Freeze Mask tool, you do want Brush Pressure to be 100%, so that you don't only *partially* protect an area. After you've adjusted the brush pressure, paint over the areas you want to protect. A red mask shows you the protected areas.

6. Slim the Belly

To remove the love handles, select the Push Left tool, and reduce the Brush Pressure to 25% again. Use a larger brush, and move it along the side of the belly in one fell swoop. Do the same for the other side. It would be great if we could do the same thing with physical flesh so easily!

7. Pucker the Gut

The sides are taken care of, but the front of the gut still pooches out. This is a job for the Pucker tool (⬚). Remember that a little goes a long way with this tool, so use it judiciously. Select the tool and then increase the size of the brush so that it's larger than the area you want to change. Reduce the Brush Pressure to 10%. Then click once to see the effect. A click or two is usually plenty.

Make any other changes you need to make to your image, and then click OK to close the Liquify dialog box.

8. Adjust Tone to Create an Illusion

You can selectively darken a portion of the abdomen, as if the light source is casting a shadow. This technique won't produce six-pack abs, but a slight shadow can make a nice difference.

First, use the Lasso tool with a feather amount of 30 pixels to select the area that should appear darker.

Then, click the Create New Adjustment Layer icon in the Layers palette, and choose Curves. The selection is automatically applied to the layer mask that's built into the Curves layer.

Command/Ctrl-click on the image where you want to darken to set a corresponding point on the curve. Then, use the up and down arrow keys to adjust the curve. Moving the point down darkens the area, creating the illusion that it's concave. Click OK to close the Curves dialog box. ▥

CHAPTER 10
Enhancing Eyes, Teeth, Hair, Lips, and Skin

©JHDAVIS

UTILIZING THE PHOTOGRAPH OF our favorite blushing bride, captured magnificently by renowned wedding photographer Brooke Christl, we return to subtle but powerful retouching techniques that can *"wow-a-fy"* an image. Focusing on certain elements of an image can make a huge difference—the difference between it looking like a snapshot or a fine-art portrait.

Here, we'll cover everything from windows to the soul (eye enhancements), to lips and teeth tricks, to creating that Hollywood glow, which, dog-gone-it, just makes everyone look utterly fantastic.

©BROOKE CHRISTL PHOTOGRAPHY

Brightening Teeth and Eyes

Polish the teeth and brighten the eyes with a simple Hue/Saturation adjustment layer.

There's a Method to the Madness.
Before you dive in to start retouching an image, think about all the changes you want to make. The order in which you edit the file determines how much flexibility you'll have, and how effects will appear.

For most portraits, the workflow I've laid out here will give you maximum flexibility. For example, reshaping the gums earlier expanded the area of the teeth. Had you polished the teeth first, brightening would have applied to only part of the final tooth area.

1. Make a Selection

A single Hue/Saturation adjustment layer can both remove stains from the teeth and brighten the whites of the eyes. You could create an adjustment layer right away, but I recommend making a selection first so that much of the layer mask, which determines where the adjustment layer affects the image, will already be in place. You can add to the layer mask later.

Use the Lasso tool with a Feather value of about 3 pixels to select the teeth. To switch to the Polygonal Lasso tool as you make the selection, press Option/Alt. Click points with the Polygonal Lasso tool, or click and drag to draw freeform shapes with the regular Lasso tool.

Draw around the teeth. The feathering gives you a little leeway so that you can use the Polygonal Lasso tool even in areas that aren't exactly straight edges.

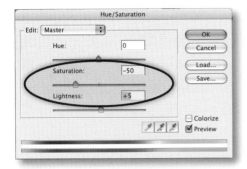

2. Add a Hue/Saturation Adjustment Layer

Click the Create New Adjustment Layer icon in the Layers palette, and choose Hue/Saturation. To remove any stains from the teeth, reduce the Saturation. How much you reduce it depends on the portrait; be careful not to go too far or you'll end up with unattractive gray teeth.

Increase the Lightness. You'll be able to fine-tune it later with a dodge-and-burn process. Right now, just increase the overall lightness. Once again, be careful not to go too far, or you'll end up with an artificial smile, or even worse, flat glow-in-the-dark teeth **A**—great for Halloween but not the desired effect in most portraits. I tend to be conservative with the Lightness and leave it at about 5. **B**

Click OK to close the Hue/Saturation dialog box.

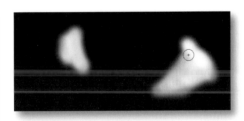

3. Mask the Areas to Brighten

Every adjustment layer comes with a layer mask, and because you selected the teeth before creating the layer mask, they're already there. Now, simply add to the mask any other areas in the image that you want to brighten with the changes you made in the Hue/Saturation dialog box.

With white as the foreground color, you may now paint over the whites of the eyes. The desaturation and lightness settings in the Hue/Saturation dialog box can remove any eye color that's being reflected in the whites or any unflattering reds that appear there.

Option/Alt-click the mask in the Layers palette to view it. You can paint directly on it to clean it up a little and make sure you've covered the areas you intended to. ▥

> ### CAUTION
>
> **Deselect Before Painting.** Any time a selection is active, changes affect only the selected area. You can paint to your heart's content anywhere else on the image and it will have no effect. Press Command/Ctrl-D to deselect quickly.

©BROOKE CHRISTI PHOTOGRAPHY

Dodge and Burn Portrait Magic

Pull out highlights, shape the shadows, and give a little extra sparkle to an image with a quick dodge-and-burn layer.

INSIGHT

Using Neutral Colors. You don't actually need to fill the layer with a neutral color to dodge and burn, as long as the blending mode is Overlay or Soft Light. However, filling the layer with the neutral color lets you see what you're doing, and it doesn't add much to the file size because PSD files are inherently compressed.

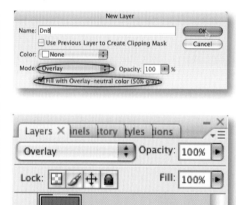

1. Apply a Blending Mode

Dodging and burning (lightening and darkening) areas of a portrait can really bring it to life. You can dodge and burn on the same layer using one of Photoshop's contrast blending modes. Creating a separate layer above your original also ensures that the changes are nondestructive.

Option/Alt-click the Create New Layer icon in the Layers palette. In the New Layer dialog box, name the layer. More important, select either the Overlay or Soft Light blending mode. Overlay is more extreme; Soft Light is more subtle. In this example, I chose Overlay because it will intensify the color in the eyes.

Select Fill With Overlay-Neutral Color (50% Gray). Until you paint on the layer, and create areas brighter or darker than 50% gray, the layer will have no effect on the underlying image at all. When you do paint on the layer, you'll be able to see where you're darkening and where you're lightening the image. Click OK to create the layer.

T I P

Exaggerate Vignetting. You can exaggerate any vignetting you added in Camera Raw by painting with black on a dodge-and-burn layer around the edges of the image. The darker the vignette, the more the eye is drawn inward to the subject of the image.

2. Paint with Black to Darken

Make sure your foreground and background colors are set to black and white. (Press D to return to the default colors if they're not there.) Use a soft paintbrush, possibly even a Hardness of 0, and reduce its Opacity quite a bit—something between 5 and 15% Opacity. Any time you're painting by hand, it's better to build up the changes than to make dramatic changes that you have to undo. Paint in the shadowy areas to darken them without losing detail.

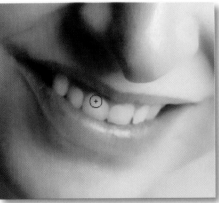

3. Paint with White to Lighten

To swap the foreground and background colors, tap the X key. Paint with white anywhere you want to lighten the image, such as the teeth, the whites of the eyes, and highlights in the hair. Even a little painting adds brightness to the eyes and the smile. If you overdo it anywhere, just paint with black over it.

You can move around the image, lightening and darkening, changing brush size and paint color as you go. Keep your finger near the X key so you can easily switch between dodging and burning.

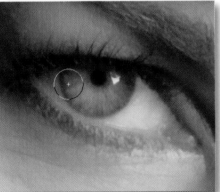

4. Lighten the Irises

They say the eyes are the windows to the soul, and they're certainly an important part of any portrait. Therefore, the irises deserve a little extra attention. One popular technique is to lighten only the portion of the iris that is opposite the main light source, so that it appears that the light is bouncing around within clear cornea that covers the iris and the pupil. Paint the same side of the other iris as well. ▥

@BROOKE CHRISTL PHOTOGRAPHY

Wow-A-Fying Pupils

In bright light, pupils contract. Expanding them gives the portrait's subject a more natural look.

1. Create a New Layer

Remember what your mother told you about people with beady eyes? Unfortunately, the bright lights we photographers often use cause pupils to contract so that the subject can appear frightened or even evil. To give the portrait's subject the benefit of the doubt, make those pupils a little larger—*without losing the specular highlights.*

Start by creating a new layer so that you can make changes to pupils without affecting anything else in the image. Click the Create New Layer icon, and name the layer Pupils.

2. Sample the Pupil Color

Pupils aren't pure black. How black they are varies from image to image. So, for realistic results, use the Eyedropper tool to sample one of the pupils and use that for the fill color in the next step.

3. Draw a Larger Pupil

Select the Elliptical Marquee tool, and set Feather to about 5 pixels, to match the softness of the real pupils.

Click in the center of a pupil, and press Option/Alt-Shift to draw a perfect circle from the center, a little bit larger than the existing pupil.

Shift the pupil selection to center it in the full iris. Press Option/Alt-Delete to fill the pupil with the foreground color, which is the color you sampled.

4. Retrieve Specular Highlights

The newly drawn pupil blocks the existing specular highlights. The most effective way to get those specular highlights back is to use the Blend If sliders.

Click the Add A Layer Style icon in the Layers palette, and choose Blending Options. In the Layer Style dialog box, go directly to the Blend If sliders.

You want to hide a portion of the current layer by giving priority to the layer that's underneath, where the specular highlights are. To bring back highlights, drag the white slider to the left until you see the detail you want. To smooth the transition, press Option/Alt and click the white slider to split it. Move the left half of the slider to the left to obtain a smooth transition.

5. Copy the Pupil

No need to repeat the entire process for the other eye. Instead, roughly select around the pupil you just created, and press Ctrl-Alt or Command-Option. Photoshop duplicates the currently selected area. Drag the duplicate to center it in the other eye. Even the specular highlights are fine. 🔲

Wow-A-Fying Lips

Bring density to the lips with a simple Blending Mode fashion trick.

T I P

Saving a Selection. To reuse a selection, save it as an alpha channel: Make the selection. Then click the Save Selection As Channel icon in the Channels palette.

To use the selection later, select it in the Channels palette, and click the Load Channel As Selection icon.

1. Isolate the Lips

The Multiply blending mode can quickly intensify the color in an image. You'll use it to add color and density to the lips. First, select the lips. Use the Lasso tool with a Feather of 3 pixels for a soft edge. Remember that you can press Option/Alt to switch to the Polygonal Lasso tool.

When the lips are selected, you need to copy them to their own layer. Remember, though, that the lips are now a combination of the original lips plus patches and adjustments on other layers. So, choose Edit > Copy Merged to copy everything that's currently visible under the selection to the clipboard. Then, choose Edit > Paste to paste to a new layer.

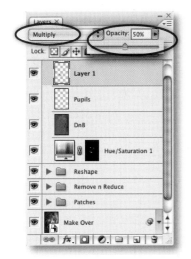

2. Change the Blending Mode

Adding density to the lips is actually quite easy, almost magical. Change the blending mode for the new "lips" layer to Multiply. The Multiply blending mode multiplies the base color (in this case, the lips on the layers below) with the lips on the new layer. This blending mode always results in a darker color.

At full opacity, this blending mode may be a little heavy-handed unless you want a film noir look. Reduce the layer's Opacity to achieve the effect you want to help tell your story.

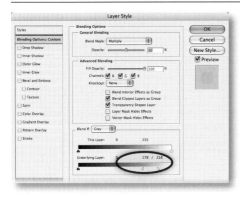

3. Retrieve Highlights

The blending mode has obscured the highlights in the lips. To bring those back, take advantage of the Blend If sliders again. You can use the same technique you used to retrieve the specular highlights in the pupils.

Click the Add A Layet Style icon in the Layers palette, and choose Blending Options. Then, in the Blend If area of the Layer Style dialog box, drag the white Underlying Layer slider to the left. Press Option/Alt and click the slider to split it. Move the left side of the slider to the left to create a smooth transition. ▥

©BROOKE CHRISTL PHOTOGRAPHY

Sharpening Selectively

Use targeted sharpening to showcase your story. Even subtle changes can make a difference in where viewers focus their attention.

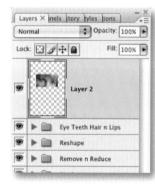

1. Isolate the Area to Sharpen

You used Camera Raw to do some base sharpening earlier. But late in the process of retouching a portrait, you'll often find it useful to sharpen specific areas of the image in Photoshop. The eyes are the key aspect of most portraits, so sharpening the eyelashes, eyebrows, and irises can make a big difference.

If you're working on a high-resolution file, and you're sharpening only a small area of your image, you can improve Photoshop's performance by selecting only the area you intend to sharpen.

Use the Lasso or Marquee tool to select the area you want to sharpen. By this point in the retouching process, the eyes include content on multiple layers. So choose Edit > Copy Merged to copy all the visible content within the selection from every layer. Then choose Edit > Paste to paste it to a new layer.

2. Apply the Unsharp Mask Filter

For most targeted sharpening, use the Unsharp Mask filter. Choose Filter > Sharpen > Unsharp Mask.

When you're working with just a portion of a portrait (like eyes and lashes), you can increase the Radius value. Unfortunately, increasing the Radius can introduce more artifacts, so keep the Amount lower than it would be for sub-pixel sharpening (below 1 pixel Radius). Move the Amount slider much higher before seeing any artifacts.

Here, with a Radius of 1.5, an Amount setting of 200% doesn't give significant edge artifacts, but it does sharpen the noise and the skin texture. That's where the Threshold slider comes in. It determines when the filter starts sharpening. Increase it until the subtleties are no longer sharpened. Specifically, keep an eye on the skin as you move the slider, Even a Threshold of 2 is a significant improvement over 0, and you can usually move it up a little higher to sharpen the areas you want without affecting the subtleties. Click OK to close the filter dialog box.

INSIGHT

Unsharp Mask vs. Smart Sharpen. Smart Sharpen is better for global sharpening. Use it in images where you want to sharpen just about everything, as in architecture, landscape, or product shots.

Unsharp Mask, with its Threshold slider, is a better option for more targeted sharpening like portraits.

3. Mask the Areas to Sharpen

With a layer mask, you can apply the sharpening to specific areas in the layer.

By default, layer masks are white. However, in this case, it's easier to *start with a black mask* and paint *in* white to reveal the underlying layers. To create a black mask, press Option/Alt as you click the Add Layer Mask icon in the Layers palette.

Now, set the foreground color to white, and use a paintbrush with about 50% opacity to paint in sharpening around the eyelashes and the irises of the eyes, the eyebrows, and possibly even every individual eyelash. Just don't paint over the whites of the eyes, because there's likely to be a little noise there that you don't want to sharpen.

Casting a Hollywood Glow

Some people refer to this as a diffuse glow or a soft glow—whatever you call it (I refer to it as the "charge more money" effect), it's a way to soften and dramatize your portrait. To create a glow, add density to the midtones and sculpt the light as it interacts with the subject of the image.

Three variations let you control the glow to get exactly the effect you want.

Subtle Glow

Start by creating a new layer with a copy of the current image. If all the data is in one layer, simply duplicate the layer. However, if you're adding this effect after retouching an image, you'll need to make a merged copy of everything currently visible.

The Merge Visible command would compress the file to a single layer, so use a handy keyboard shortcut instead. There isn't even a corresponding menu command for this shortcut, which is affectionately known as elbow+E because you basically just press your elbow across the corner of your keyboard and press E. To use the shortcut more precisely, press Command-Option-Shift-E (Mac OS) or Ctrl-Alt-Shift-E (Windows). Name the new layer Glow.

Now, choose Filter > Blur > **Surface Blur.** The Surface Blur filter lets you blur unnecessary detail while keeping areas of contrast sharp.

In the Surface Blur dialog box, adjust the Radius and Threshold sliders to soften the skin tone of the image while keeping a fair amount of the detail intact. Try 15 and 15 to start.

Next, change the blending mode to **Soft Light** to recover some additional detail. Soft Light is one of the contrast blending modes, which can both lighten the light areas and darken the shadows.

If you've lost shadow detail you want to retain, bring it back using the Blend If sliders. Click the Add Layer Style icon in the Layers palette, and then choose Blending Options.

Use **the Blend If sliders** to hide the shadows in the current layer: Slide the black triangle in the This Layer slider to the right until you see the shadow detail again. The black slider determines at what point the layer becomes invisible on a Luminosity scale from 0 to 255.

Then Option/Alt-click the slider to split it, and drag the two halves apart to achieve a smooth transition. Try the split black sliders at 50/150 to start.

This technique added some light, added some drama, and boosted saturation. You can now adjust the Glow layer's Opacity to determine the extent of the glow.

Gaussian Glow

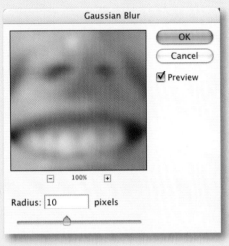

For a stronger glow, use the **Gaussian Blur** filter instead of the Surface Blur filter.

Starting with your image without a glow layer, use the keyboard shortcut to copy the merged visible layers onto a new layer (Command-Option-Shift-E in Mac OS or Ctrl-Alt-Shift–E in Windows), and call that layer Gaussian Glow. Change the blending mode to **Soft Light** right away, before you've even run the filter, so that you can preview the final effects as you work in the Gaussian Blur dialog box.

Choose Filter > Blur > Gaussian Blur. Start with a 10-pixel Radius and adjust it however you like. The preview in the dialog box shows the effect of the blur in Normal mode; the preview in the image window displays the image with both the blur and the changed blending mode applied.

I like to blur the image enough that the surface edges are rounded, giving more depth to the image—but not so much that I can't see the detail. How much blur you use depends on the effect you want to achieve, what's going on in the portrait, and the resolution of the file.

To pull some of the shadow detail back in, **use the Blend If sliders again**. Click the Add Layer Style icon in the Layers palette, and then choose Blending Options to open the Layer Style dialog box.

In the Blend If area of the dialog box, move the dark triangle on the This Layer slider to the right until you can see the shadow detail you want. Then, Option/Alt-click the slider to split it, and move the slider halves apart to create a smooth transition.

Dramatic Glow

When people refer to a Hollywood glow or a diffuse glow, this is often the look they mean. Blurring for a romantic appearance, this glow is popular in high school yearbooks, glamour shots, and wedding photography.

This look is just a more extreme version of the Gaussian glow. Use the Gaussian Blur filter and the Blend If sliders in just the same way, but use the **Overlay blending mode** for the blurred layer instead of the Soft Light mode. The Overlay blending mode significantly changes the saturation and contrast of the image.

When you use the Overlay blending mode, you may also need to desaturate the layer a bit (or a lot). Apply an adjustment layer that affects only the blur layer: Option/Alt-click the Create New Adjustment Layer icon, and choose Hue/Saturation. In the New Layer dialog box, select **Use Previous Layer To Create Clipping Mask.**

Then, reduce the Saturation value. To keep the glow but remove all color change, set it to –100. For a little more oomph, try moving the Saturation slider to about –60. 🖐

CHAPTER 11
Replacing, Removing, and Repairing

©J.H.DAVIS

WHEN ONE IMAGE ALONE just doesn't succeed in telling the whole story, it would be helpful to be able to show a series of prints or slides to convey your message. But in reality, you're usually given just one shot to tell a specific story.

With CS3 came the Auto Align and Auto Blend improvements to Adobe's Photomerge stitching technology, and for the first time, creating awe-inspiring panoramas (even from images taken with hand-helds) became practically automatic and instantaneous. The idea that these technologies could *also* be used for challenges such as assembling seamless group portraits and helping remove glare on glasses was the pièce de résistance!

Throw in the merging magic tricks of the improved Vanishing Point and you have the makings of an entire Vegas act that would make even Criss Angel ask, *"Wow, how'd you do that?"*

137

Stitching Together a Panorama

The Photomerge feature automatically aligns, blends, and even adjusts perspective in a series of photos to create one seamless, mind-bogglingly cool panoramic image.

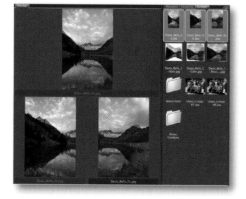

1. Apply Photomerge

If you want to create a panorama, let the Photomerge feature do the heavy lifting. Start in Bridge, and select the photos you want to stitch together. You can select them in any order; Photomerge is smart enough to sort them out. The images can be vertical, horizontal, or even a patchwork of images. When you've selected the images, choose Tools > Photoshop > Photomerge.

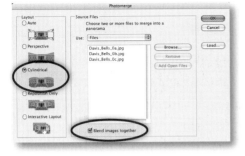

2. Select a Merge Option

In the Photomerge dialog box, select Blend Images Together. Then select an option for Photomerge to use when combining images. Depending on the angle of the lens and how close you were to your subject, you'll usually get the best results with Cylindrical.

Perspective bends the panorama around the viewer. *Cylindrical* lets Photomerge correct for lens distortion. *Reposition Only* overlaps the images, but does not distort or adjust perspective—it works best if you've shot the images from a distance and with a level tripod. *Interactive Layout* lets you adjust the position of the images yourself.

Click OK. Photoshop copies the images into a single Photoshop document, aligns them, and blends the colors and tones at the overlap. Depending on the option you selected, it may distort the images to align them, and it will create masks to hide portions of each image. It also matches the exposure and the white balance across the images—extraordinary!

INSIGHT

Omitting Objects. If an unwanted car drove through one of your shots, or your subject changed position, make sure the object you don't want—whether it's a vehicle or a person in an unfortunate pose—doesn't end up in the final panorama. Simply select and delete that object from the image before you run Photomerge or its components, Auto-Align Layers and Auto-Blend Layers.

3. Crop the Image

When Photoshop realigns the images, the edges of the new document are likely to be irregular. Select the Crop tool, and then select the area of the document you want to retain. Double-click to accept the crop.

If there is no *Background* layer in the document, you can hide, rather than delete, the area outside of your crop, so that you can change the cropping later. Select Hide in the Options bar before you double-click. Later, if you want to change the cropping, choose Image > Reveal All to see the whole thing. (The Hide option isn't available if there is a *Background* layer, because the layer called *Background* doesn't support transparency.)

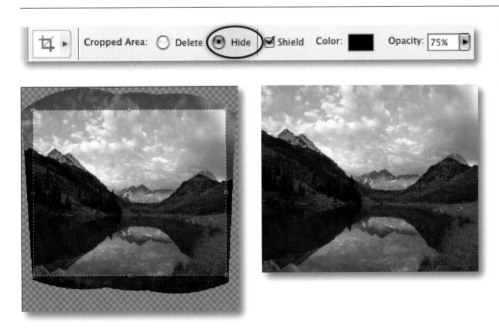

Assembling a Group Portrait

If it seems impossible to get everyone to smile at once, don't fret. Take multiple shots, and use each person's best look for the final composite.

1. Open the Images in Photoshop

You don't want to use Photomerge for a group shot, because you aren't blending a panorama. But Photoshop's Auto-Align Layers command will come in handy. Start by opening each version of your group shot as a separate layer in a single Photoshop document.

There's a quick way to open multiple images as separate layers in Photoshop. Our good friend Russell Brown provides a free tool to do just that. If you've installed Dr. Brown's Services, select the images in Bridge, and then choose Tools > Dr. Brown's Services > Dr. Brown's Merge-a-Matic. Presto! You've got your layers in Photoshop.

▶ *Download the latest version of Dr. Brown's Services free from the link at adventuresinphotoshop.com.*

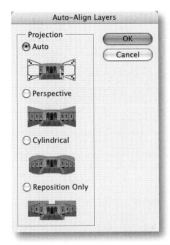

2. Align the Layers

Unless you shot the group photos with a high-quality tripod, the images probably shifted a little. First, Shift-click to select both layers (or all layers depending on how many shots you needed) in the Layers palette, and choose Edit > Auto-Align Layers.

Select an alignment option. The options are similar to those in the Photomerge dialog box. For most group shots, the movement between images is subtle, so Auto works well. Click OK. The Auto-Align Layers feature rotates and distorts the images as needed to align them.

3. Mask to Combine Images

Decide which image you consider the primary shot. That is, determine which one would require the fewest changes. Usually that's the shot in which more people are smiling or looking at the camera or standing still or dancing around—whatever your priority is for the story you're trying to tell.

Select the main image, and then click the Add Layer Mask icon.

Make sure the foreground color is black, and select the Brush tool. Use a fairly soft brush at 100% opacity to paint wherever you want the secondary image beneath to show through. As you paint, you're punching a hole in one photo to reveal the image below.

INSIGHT

Beyond Group Shots. Use this technique whenever you want to replace one portion of a shot with another. For example, paint a darker exposure into a lighter exposure of the same scene.

Where odd transitions occurred because people shifted between shots, make the brush a little *softer* or reduce its opacity to fade one image into another. You may also need to reduce the size of the brush in some places to ensure that you replace only the people you're targeting, and not their neighbors; also, you may need to use a harder brush to minimize the edge transition from one person to another. Of course, if you need to backtrack, remember that you can undo areas of your mask by painting in white. Press X to swap the foreground and background colors. 🎨

Patching a Background

If a light post, palm frond, or anything else is distracting the viewer from your story, get rid of it! Use the Clone Stamp tool, dodge and burn techniques, and a little ingenuity to clear the air.

See page 27 to learn how to locate this book's follow-along images, cinematic tutorials, downloadable freebies, and useful links!

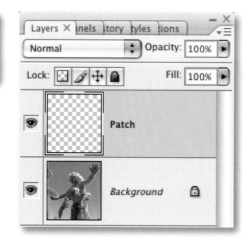

1. Create a New Layer

To protect your original pixels, make a patch layer and implement your fixes on it. Click the Create A New Layer icon in the Layers palette to add a layer, and then name it Patch. Don't let the name mislead you—you won't be needing the Patch tool. Or the Healing Brush tool, for that matter. Both of those tools blend patched areas with their background. When you want to remove an object, you want to *remove* it, not leave a smudge in its place. So get ready to use the Clone Stamp tool instead.

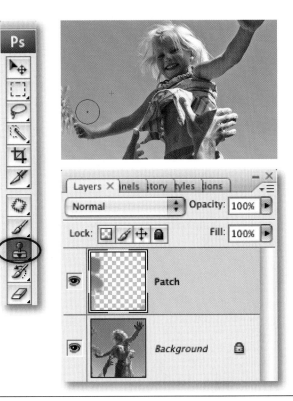

2. Replace the Distractions

To use the Clone Stamp tool, you sample an area you want to use as the source, and then you paint over the area you want to replace. That's perfect if you want to replace a palm frond, for example, with sky that looks just like the sky around it.

Select the Clone Stamp tool. Keep it large, with a soft edge. In fact, set the Hardness to 0, because you want to get rid of the distraction, not just fade it. Set the Opacity to 100%.

Make sure the new layer you created is active. Option/Alt-click to select a source point, and then paint over the area you want to remove. If the distraction is close to overlapping an area of the image you want to keep, don't fuss with it. Go ahead and paint over the distraction. You can repair the area later.

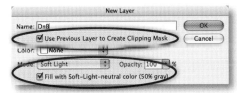

3. Dodge and Burn the Patch Layer

To smooth out the tonal irregularities between your patch and the background, create a dodge and burn layer that affects only the patch layer: Option/Alt-click the Create New Layer icon in the Layers palette to open the New Layer dialog box. Name the layer, and change the blending mode to *Soft Light* so that you can darken and lighten on the same layer. Select *Fill With Soft-Light-neutral-color (50% Gray)* so that you can see what you're doing. Then, select *Use Previous Layer To Create Clipping Mask* so that this layer will affect only the layer directly below it. Click OK. The arrow in the layer thumbnail shows you that it affects only the patch layer below it.

Select the Brush tool with a large, soft brush, and reduce its opacity to about 5%. Paint with black where you want to darken the layer and paint with white where you want to lighten it.

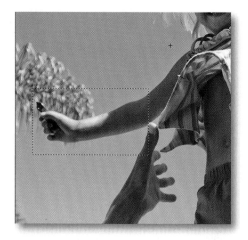

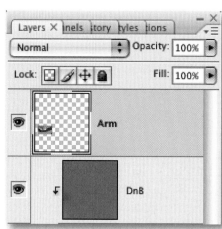

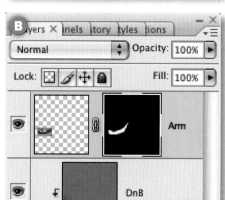

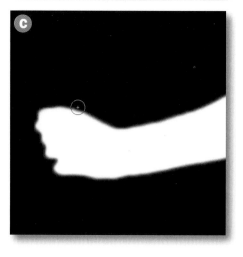

4. Repair Any Damage

Now it's time to bring back any portion of the original image that you sacrificed for expediency in removing the distracting elements. The undamaged area is all still there on the first layer. So click on the first layer.

Then, select the area that includes the portion you want to recover with the Marquee tool. For example, in this image, select the entire arm so that the hand is in place. Then choose Layer > New > Layer Via Copy to copy it to its own layer. Move that new layer to the top of the stack and name it.

Next, you'll mask to reveal only the portion you want to protect. Select the Quick Select tool. You don't need to select Auto Enhance. Just drag over the area you want to recover. For a more precise selection, click Refine Edge. The default settings for Refine Edge may be a little heavy-handed, so make any adjustments you need to do the job.

Now, with the marching ants on the screen indicating your selection A, click the Add Layer Mask icon. Photoshop uses your selection as a basis for the mask B. Now that area of the original image appears above the other layers. If you end up with a little halo, or otherwise need to tidy the edge a bit, use the Dodge and Burn tools. Use the Burn tool with Shadows selected in the Options bar to darken the edge of the mask shadows C; use the Dodge tool with Highlights selected in the Options bar to lighten the mask edge. The tools affect only the layer mask, nothing beneath it. ▥

Removing Glare from Glasses

Get past the glare in eyeglasses to see the eyes behind them—even if you have to cheat a little bit.

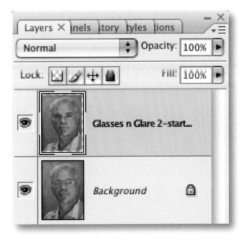

1. Open Images in Photoshop

Eyes reveal a subject's personality, but they're often obscured by eyeglass glare. There are different ways to remove that glare, but the easiest one is to borrow the eyes from another image. So, if at all possible, take two shots of your subject: one with glasses and one without, even if they're slightly different poses. All you need are the eyes.

Then open the images as separate layers in a Photoshop document. To do that quickly, choose Tools > Dr. Brown's Services > Dr. Brown's Merge-A-Matic, and click OK to let the tool open a new Photoshop document with your layers in place. Make sure your glass lens layer is on top.

▶ *If you don't have Dr. Brown's Services, download them for free from the link at adventuresinphotoshop.com.*

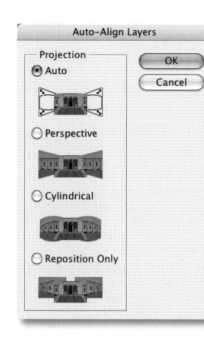

2. Align the Images

Shift-click to select both layers, and choose Edit > Auto-Align Layers. Select Auto, and click OK. How well this feature works for you depends on the differences in the poses. Photoshop doesn't know that the eyes are your priority, so typically it works to align the background and other stationary aspects of the image instead.

To see how well the eyes line up, change the blending mode of the top layer to Difference. This blending mode shows you where the layers differ (the color areas) and where they are identical, (the blacks). Shift the eyes in one image to match the other. It can be a bit tricky because the glasses change the eyes, but you can usually get it very close. When you've aligned the eyes, change the blending mode back to Normal.

3. Mask the Glasses

You'll create a mask so that you can drop the eyes from the other image into the glasses. Use the Lasso tool with a Feather of 1 pixel to select just inside the edge of the glasses. Press Option/Alt to switch to the Polygonal Lasso tool as you make the selection. Be sure to select around any metal areas or any other decorative areas of the glasses.

TIP

Moving the Mask. By default, the mask is linked to the image. If you need to shift it independently, click the link icon to unlink it.

With the selection active, select the top layer that doesn't have glasses. Then click the Add Layer Mask icon. Photoshop uses the selection to create the mask. Presto. The glare is gone.

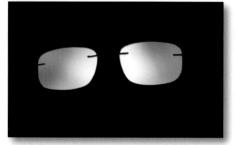

4. Paint in Reflection

The glasses don't look realistic with no reflection at all. Paint in black on the mask where you want the reflection to appear. Use a large paintbrush with a lowered opacity, say 30%. For realistic glasses, paint in a little reflection on the corners. You'll get the reflection without hiding the eyes.

Smoothing Color Banding

Eliminate color banding, or posterizing, with the Healing Brush tool.

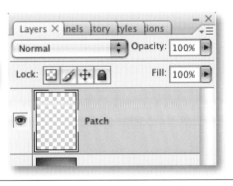

1. Create a New Layer

Banding occurs when the color or tone of the image is out of ***gamut*** (a reproducible range), typically in photos that contain very bright elements or that are shot at night, in low light, or that are oversaturated. To smooth the banding into a gradient, open the image in Photoshop. Then click the Create New Layer icon to add a patch layer.

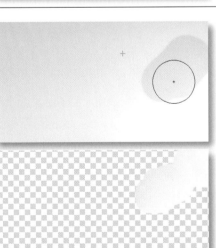

2. Heal the Banding

Select the Healing Brush tool. In the Options bar, set a hard edge; a softer brush would hurt the result. Select Current And Below from the Sample menu so that you can pick up samples from the layer below. Deselect Aligned so you can sample from one area to perform all the fixes, possible because the tool uses mostly texture, not color and tone.

Option/Alt-click a representative noise area to sample it, and then paint in short strokes over the band.

You couldn't ask for an easier fix! ▥

©JHDAVIS

Patching Highlight Detail

If detail is blown out of a portion of your image, try painting just enough of the detail back in.

1. Copy an Area with Detail

When a single exposure won't let you capture both shadow and highlight details, it's best to take multiple exposures and merge the information. But sometimes it just isn't possible to take multiple exposures, as in action shots. As long as you've captured detail in a similar part of the image, you may be able to do a little copying and pasting to create believable, subtle detail where it's been lost.

Start by identifying the detail that would work. For example, in this image, the area just below the duck's neck is blown out, but its feathers would be similar to detail a little farther down.

Use the Lasso tool with a feather of 10 pixels to grab a likely area. Choose Edit > New > Layer Via Copy. Photoshop puts the selection on a new layer.

2. Transform the Patch

Choose Edit > Free Transform. Then move the patch to the blown-out area and rotate, scale, or warp it to fit it into the space appropriately. One patch probably won't do the trick, so don't expect it to fill the entire area—just try to align it. Click the Commit button or double-click to accept the position.

3. Position Additional Patches

Press Command/Ctrl-J to make another copy of the patch layer. Then press Command/Ctrl-T to access the Free Transform command, and drag the new patch into position. Double-click to accept it. Continue adding patch layers and moving them into position until you've built up the texture you need and have filled the blown-out area.

If you need to manipulate the patch more extensively than simply rotating or scaling it, click the Warp mode icon **A**, and then move portions of the grid **B** to warp the patch appropriately.

4. Reduce the Opacity

In most cases, the patches won't automatically appear natural, especially if they've all been replicated from the same original selection. You just need enough detail that the eye perceives the image exposure as accurate, so blend the patches in a bit more.

First, Shift-click to select all the layers in the Layers palette, and then choose New Group From Layers in the Layers palette menu. Grouping layers keeps the Layers palette tidy, but it also lets you make changes to all the members of a group at once.

Change the Opacity of the Group to about 50% and then tweak it for your image. The opacity of all the layers changes at once.

5. Mask Extraneous Patching

If patches have overlapped the edge of your background object, or otherwise slipped out of the area you're patching, you can hide the extraneous portion by adding a layer mask to an entire group.

Select the group, and then click the Add Layer Mask icon. Use the Brush tool, with black as the foreground color, to paint over any stray areas of the patches.

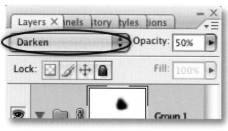

6. Change the Blending Mode

To make the patched area less conspicuous, change the blending mode for the group. Use Darken to ensure that the patches can only darken, not lighten, any area you've patched—important when you're bringing detail to a bright area that's been clipped.

> **TIP**
>
> **Opacity Shortcuts.** If a *brush tool* is selected, pressing a *number key* on the keyboard changes the opacity of the *tool*. Otherwise, the number keys change the *opacity of the selected layer*. Press 2 for 20% opacity, 5 for 50%, and so on.

7. Fine-tune Opacity

You can also fine-tune the opacity for each layer, so more detail shows in some areas than others, imitating the way light hits the subject: Expand the Group in the Layers palette. Then apply different opacity values to each layer. In this image, we've made the top layer, at the neck, 30% opaque, and the next one down 40%, the next 50%, and so on, so there's a subtle transition between what's visible and what's not.

8. Add Patches as Necessary

You can add patches until you're happy with the result. You can add patches that are outside of any group, to give you more flexibility. Try using the Healing Brush tool to sample from another part of the image and paint, breaking up any structure you might have created accidentally. How much you need to paint depends on the image, the area that's lost detail, and the story you're telling. ▨

Retouching and Overlaying in Perspective

Traditionally, retouching objects that are in perspective—that is, not facing the camera full-on—has been tricky. Now, though, the enhanced Vanishing Point filter makes it possible to account for an object's angle (or any angle for that matter) and retouch it realistically.

About Vanishing Point

IMAGE COURTESY OF ISTOCK.COM © WILL SELAREP #2332630

Use Vanishing Point to edit an image that contains planes in perspective—such as the walls of a building, a sloping floor, or any rectangular object. First, you define the planes in an image, and then you edit it by painting, cloning, copying, pasting, or transforming. The edits are oriented and scaled to the perspective of the plane you're modifying.

You can also add textures or images that wrap around the planes you've specified, as we have here with U.S. currency.

You can continue working on your image in Photoshop after you've made edits in Vanishing Point.

Create a new empty layer before you open Vanishing Point, so that retouching occurs on its own layer, leaving your original intact.

To open Vanishing Point, choose Filter > Vanishing Point.

Defining a Plane

The first step is to define a plane. Select the Create Plane tool. Then, click the four corners of the plane in the image. The corners of the plane may not match the corners of the object in the image perfectly—the plane may extend beyond the object, for example, if it's overlapped by another plane, such as a roof. Or, if the corners of the object aren't perfectly square, the corners of the plane may not match up. Because your goal is to match the perspective, it's okay if the corners aren't a precise match with the image.

Vanishing Point helps you create a viable plane. When you click to make the fourth corner, Vanishing Point automatically switches to the Edit Plane tool and displays a grid in red, yellow, or blue. Red means trouble, an impossible plane. Yellow indicates that the plane is invalid **A**, but you might be able to get away with it. Blue means the edges are parallel and you're good to go **B**. Drag the corner handles until the grid is blue, so your edits will be properly scaled and oriented.

Creating Related Planes

You can create (tear off) additional planes that share the same vanishing point perspective as the original plane. New planes tear off at 90° angles, but you can adjust them to any angle.

You can make seamless edge transitions using related planes, such as applying a texture across the multiple walls.

To tear off a plane, Command/Ctrl-drag an edge node (looks like an anchor point in Curves) of the original plane's bounding box.

To change the angle of the plane, change the value in the Angle box in the Options bar, or Option/Alt-drag the center edge node on the side of the plane that is opposite the axis of rotation C.

You can tear additional planes off the new plane. However, once you create a new plane from an existing plane, you can no longer adjust the angle of the first plane.

Retouching in Perspective

You can edit objects in the Vanishing Point dialog box using many of the same techniques you use in the full Photoshop window, and similar tools.

The Marquee tool D makes selections and moves or clones selections.

The Stamp tool E paints with a sample of the image.

The Brush tool F paints with the color you've selected.

The Transform tool G scales, rotates, and moves a floating selection. It's similar to the Free Transform tool.

The Eyedropper tool H samples colors.

The Measure tool I measures distances and angles.

The Zoom tool J zooms in and out.

The Hand tool K moves the image in the preview window.

To copy an object, such as a window, use the Stamp tool. Option/Alt-click to set the origin point L. Then paint over the area where you want the copied object to appear M. Vanishing Point paints it in perspective so that, for example, a window gets smaller as the plane recedes N.

When you use the Stamp tool, you can choose an option from the Healing menu. To blend strokes with the surrounding content, choose On; to blend with only the lighting of the surrounding pixels, choose Luminance; to prevent the pixels from blending at all, choose Off. On is usually the best option. Select Aligned to sample pixels continuously.

When you're done editing, click OK to close the Vanishing Point dialog box. Photoshop remembers the geometry, and places your changes on their own layer.

Adding Texture to a 3D Object

Masking a 3D Object

You can add textures or graphics to a three-dimensional object using Vanishing Point. The texture or graphic will follow the contours of the planes you've created.

Next, create a new layer (in addition to the retouching you have already completed), so that the changes will be nondestructive and can be manipulated later.

First, select the texture or graphic layer and choose Select All > Edit > Copy to copy it to the clipboard **O**. The only way to bring additional content into Vanishing Point is through the clipboard; there is no import feature.

Now choose Filter > Vanishing Point.

Create any planes you want to fill with the graphic or texture, if they aren't already defined. Vanishing Point retains the geometry within the file. Since we just created planes for the entire house, we're all set.

Before you add the graphic, plan your approach. Where planes aren't related, textures are applied on top of each other and will overlap. Where planes overlap but *don't* share an edge—that is, they weren't

created by dragging out a plane from an existing one, make sure you paste the graphic first on the **back-most plane** (or "**layer**" if it helps you keep it clear in your mind), as we did with the hundred-dollar-bill texture **P**.

Press Command/Ctrl-V to paste the graphic. Then drag it over the panel you want to paste into. Press Command/Ctrl-T to access the Transform tool, and then scale and rotate it to fit the plane.

To paste the same graphic again, repeat the process as needed, working back-to-front to another plane **Q**. The graphic follows the perspective of each plane, and where planes are torn off from each other, you can wrap it around from one plane to another **R**.

If you discover that you pasted the graphic into planes in the wrong order, paste it again in the right order.

Click OK to accept the changes in Vanishing Point and return to Photoshop. You may now change the opacity of this layer if you want to allow some of the original image to show through the texture **S**.

If the planes you created in Vanishing Point don't precisely match the corners in your image, use a layer mask to tidy things up.

Use the Lasso tool with some feathering to select the object in Photoshop. Then select the layer with Vanishing Point changes, and click the Add Layer Mask icon.

Photoshop creates a layer mask in the shape of the selection, and voilà—the edges are clean **T**. 🔳

TIP

Layer for Flexibility. Because you created a new layer for the Vanishing Point edits, you can apply blending modes, adjust the Opacity, and apply Layer Styles to fine-tune the effects of the edits.

The aim of art is to represent not the outward appearance of things, but their inward significance.

—ARISTOTLE

©JHDAVIS

ENHANCING & EMBELLISHING

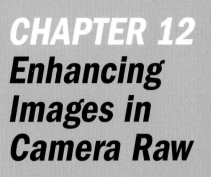

CHAPTER 12
Enhancing Images in Camera Raw

©JHDAVIS

IF YOU HAVEN'T CAUGHT ON BY NOW that ACR changes the foundation of every function you perform in your creative workflow (even to the point that you may not even *need* Photoshop for a large portion of your image work), you will by the end of this chapter!

Going beyond the captured moment to crafting what was *experienced* (or what you want your audience to experience), whether gazing at a sunset, a loved one, or a client's product, should be the goal whenever enhancing an image.

Enhancing is what you do *after* you've optimized a photograph to be the best it can be in terms of color, tone, and distraction removal. It's the icing on the cake, the presentation of the plate, the sauce that "makes" the dish.

©JHDAVIS

Creative White Balance and Retouching in ACR

Don't be afraid to take a few liberties with color temperature and tint to help tell your story.

1. Optimize the Tone of the Image

Always optimize an image before you enhance it in Camera Raw. First, click Auto to set the Exposure and Black points. Next, adjust the Brightness and Contrast sliders, then the Fill Light and Recovery, if needed. Finally, adjust the Clarity and Vibrance sliders.

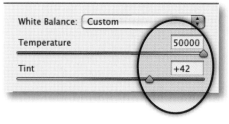

2. Set the White Balance

Because the white balance isn't permanently assigned to the file when you shoot a raw image, you can change its setting (and thus the photo's mood) later. Start by trying the options in the White Balance menu of the Basic panel. For example, Cloudy works as a starting point for this sunset image. Next, adjust the Temperature and Tint sliders.

White Balance menu options aren't available for JPEG or TIFF images because whatever was set in the camera was "burned" into the file when you pressed the shutter, though you can still use the Temperature and Tint sliders to create a Custom White Balance.

Clarity	70
Vibrance	+81
Saturation	+17

3. Increase the Vibrance and Saturation

For most projects, I encourage you to avoid the Saturation slider. When you're exaggerating the white balance, though, increased saturation in conjunction with a high Vibrance setting can intensify the mood. For this sunset, saturation is a must. So try increasing the saturation to see how far you can push it for your image.

Lens Vignetting

| Amount | -76 |
| Midpoint | 16 |

4. Add a Vignette

To add a little oomph around the edges of the file and draw the eye into the center of the composition, add a vignette. In the Lens Correction panel, adjust the Lens Vignetting sliders. Move the Amount slider to the left to darken the vignette. The Midpoint slider determines how far in the darkening comes.

TIP

Retouch in Camera Raw. ACR's Retouch tool isn't nearly as robust as the Healing Brush and other tools in Photoshop, but it's sufficient to remove a spot or two. In this image we broke all the rules and experimented with how far we could push retouching in ACR. My suggestion: Do this in Photoshop! If you want to try such an intensive retouching job, don't let your source circles overlap because the order of healing changes each time you open the file!

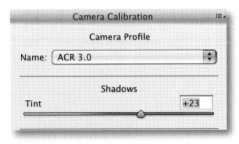

Camera Calibration

Camera Profile

Name: ACR 3.0

Shadows

| Tint | +23 |

5. Neutralize or Exaggerate Shadows

Camera Raw has one more tool you can use to enhance the color mood of the image. It's in an unlikely spot: the Camera Calibration panel. The Shadows slider affects the color of the shadows independently of any color in the image, so you can actually tint them toward green or magenta for effect. For the sunset in this image, exaggerating the color already in the shadow further dramatizes the scene.

©JHDAVIS

Tinting for an Antiqued Look

Transform a full-color image to look like an antique tinted photograph, either as a straight sepia tone or one with colors from the original, but subdued.

Brightness	+64
Contrast	+78
Clarity	60
Vibrance	+61

1. Optimize the Image

As always, optimize the image in Camera Raw before you make any enhancements. Even if you're going to convert an image to grayscale, it's best to adjust the tone first. Start by cropping the image to remove any distractions from your primary subject. Then, click Auto to set the black and white points; adjust the Brightness and Contrast sliders; and adjust the Clarity and Vibrance sliders. (Don't use Clarity on a real portrait, as it emphasizes skin flaws, but with this image of a Marilyn Monroe figure, it's fine.)

HTW **See page 27** to learn how to locate this book's follow-along images, cinematic tutorials, downloadable freebies, and useful links!

2. Convert to Grayscale

Click the HSL/Grayscale tab. Then select the Convert To Grayscale option. All the colors are neutralized.

3. Adjust the Colors and Tones

Click Auto. For this image, Camera Raw automatically creates an S curve that darkens the yellows, lightens the blues, and adjusts the reds. You can then adjust the colors further. Because the yellow hair separates the figure from the background, I might brighten the yellows and decrease the oranges of the skin tones.

Whenever you're making these kinds of adjustments, zoom in to make sure you won't end up with unwanted noise.

4. Add a Tint

Select the Split-Toning tab. Use the Shadows adjustments in this panel, and stay away from the Highlights adjustments. Increase Saturation until you start to see color. Then, select the Hue you want to use. Move the Balance slider to the left to include color in the highlights or to the right to color only the shadows **A**.

To use some of the image's original color along with the sepia tone, deselect Convert To Grayscale in the HSL/Grayscale panel. Then, in the Basic panel, reduce the Vibrance, which leaves a little bit of color in the file even at 0. And the sepia or other split-tone color is still there **B**.

5. Add a Vignette

As you know by now, I'm a big believer in using vignettes to lead the eye into an image and in this case, also add to the antiqued appearance. Select the Lens Correction tab, and move the Amount and Midpoint sliders to taste. The Midpoint determines how much the vignette transitions into the image.

As you adjust the sliders, keep in mind that the vignette is set in relationship to the *full* image, not the cropped area.

©JHDAVIS

Selective "Hand Recoloring" in ACR

You don't have to choose: Part of the photo can be in color, and part in black-and-white. Selectively desaturate or resaturate colors to create compelling images.

1. Optimize the Image

Once again, get the tone right before enhancing the image. You can spend time tweaking all the settings, but for most images, the usual four-step process works well.

First, crop out any distractions. Then, click Auto to set your Exposure and Black sliders, adjust the Brightness and Contrast sliders, and adjust the Clarity and Vibrance sliders. Use Clarity sparingly if you're working with a portrait, as it can emphasize skin blemishes and other minor flaws.

	Auto	Default
Exposure		+0.30
Recovery		0
Fill Light		0
Blacks		4
Brightness		+48
Contrast		+38
Clarity		0
Vibrance		0
Saturation		0

Reds	-100
Oranges	-100
Yellows	-100
Greens	-100
Aquas	-100
Blues	-100
Purples	-100
Magentas	-100

2. Desaturate All the Colors

Select the HSL/Grayscale tab. Then, select the Saturation tab. Drag all the sliders to −100 to desaturate all the colors. The image appears to be grayscale, but it's not.

Instead of dragging all the sliders manually, you can quickly desaturate an image using one of the How to Wow presets mentioned on page 43. If you've installed the presets, just select the Presets tab, and then click the How-c-HSL Desat preset. All the sliders move to −100 automatically.

HSL / Grayscale

☐ Convert to Grayscale

Hue | Saturation | Luminance

Default

Reds	-50
Oranges	-100
Yellows	-100
Greens	0
Aquas	-24
Blues	-53
Purples	-100
Magentas	-46

3. Add Saturation Selectively

Now, decide which colors you want to restore. For an image like this one, you can color only the flowers—both petals and stems—by resaturating the reds, greens, aquas, and blues (which are reflected from the sky). Which colors you saturate depends entirely on the subject of your image and the story you're telling.

For even more control, you can adjust the hue and the luminance for each color.

Keep in mind that skin tones are mainly orange, for any ethnicity. So to lighten the skin tone, adjust the Oranges slider in the Luminance tab. Leave the Oranges slider alone to retain the skin tone as it is.

4. Add a Vignette

Draw the eye in to the color you've featured by adding a vignette. Select the Lens Correction tab. Then, adjust the Amount. Use a higher value for the midpoint to create a vignette close to the edge. If you need to go back into the Basic panel to fine-tune the image's global brightness and contrast, go right ahead. ▦

©iStockPhoto

Exaggerated Illustrated Edge and Tone Technique in ACR

Give a photograph the exaggerated edges and tonal details of an illustration. You have everything you need to create the look instantly in Camera Raw.

1. Move Four Sliders to 100%

Start the process in the Basic panel. Move the Recovery slider all the way to 100% to increase the highlight detail. Then, move the Fill Light slider to 100% to pull out the detail in the shadows. Next, move the Contrast slider to 100% to exaggerate the midtones. Finally, move the Clarity slider to 100% to provide even greater edge detail.

You can fine-tune any of these adjustments at any time, but don't do it yet.

2. Reduce the Vibrance

Now, flatten the image's color by moving the Vibrance slider to the left. Start at −100 and then adjust it to taste. Lowering the Vibrance setting makes the image look more like a faded illustration or a watercolor painting. The high level of detail in the subject also contributes to the illustration effect.

Exposure		+0.15
Recovery		100
Fill Light		100
Blacks		24
Brightness		+3

3. Adjust Three Sliders to Taste

Next, adjust Exposure, Blacks, and Brightness for your image. Exposure sets the white point; Blacks sets the black point; and Brightness affects the midtones. How you set the sliders depends on the tone of your original image. Consider increasing the Blacks setting quite a bit to further exaggerate the contrast in the file.

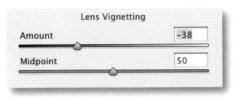

Lens Vignetting		
Amount		-38
Midpoint		50

4. Add a Vignette

Exaggerate the image's edges with a vignette. On the Lens Correction panel, adjust the Amount and Midpoint sliders to darken the edges of the image.

Detail		
Sharpening		
Amount		150
Radius		3.0
Detail		14
Masking		45
Noise Reduction		
Luminance		100
Color		100

5. Sharpen the Image

You could stop there, but to further intensify the effect, oversharpen the image. First, zoom in to 100% so you can see the effects of your settings. Then, on the Detail panel, move the Radius slider up and adjust the Amount to taste. To really exaggerate the sharpening, take the Amount slider all the way up to 150%. Leave the Detail slider low to avoid adding artifacts and pixelization. Move the Masking slider to the right to restrict the sharpening to the edges. To see where sharpening will occur, press Option/Alt as you drag the Masking slider.

If your ACR adjustments have added noise to the file, use the Noise Reduction sliders to minimize it. In fact, moving the Luminance and Color sliders all the way to the right increases the illustration effect. The noise reduction sliders soften the detail, making the image appear painted. ▥

T I P

Save as a Preset. If you want to enhance other images the same way, save your final settings as a preset by going to the Presets panel and clicking on the page icon in the lower right. Then you can apply the preset once to each image, and make only slight variations as necessary. You'll find your preset in Bridge by right-clicking on any JPEG, raw, or unlayered TIFF file and selecting Develop Settings, and finding your preset in the pop-out list.

CHAPTER 13
Edge, Glow, Overlay, and Blurring Effects

©JHDAVIS

WITH ADOBE'S CREATIVE SUITE, we have a wealth of creative options at our fingertips. With Layers, Filters (especially Smart ones), Blend Modes, and Overlays we have the ability to be *expressive* with how we shape our work of art or creative communication.

From illustrative looks to graduated neutral density filter effects, and from custom "grunge" texture overlays to creative use of focus and blurs, having these techniques at our disposal can set our images apart from the deluge of repetitive visuals we see daily. With those, along with the entire "bat utility belt" of other techniques in this book, we can specifically shape an image in order to strengthen the story that our work was created to convey.

©HDAVIS

Creating an Exaggerated Tone and Edge Effect in Photoshop

Exaggerate the edges in a photograph to make the image look like an illustration. Use Smart Objects to keep the changes nondestructive.

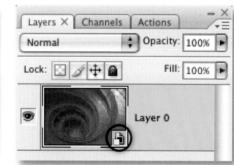

1. Open the Image as a Smart Object

To make the changes nondestructively, so you can edit them at any time, open the image as a Smart Object from Camera Raw, or take an existing image in Photoshop, right-click its Layers palette, and choose Convert To Smart Object. A Smart Object icon appears in its thumbnail in the Layers palette.

2. Apply Shadows/Highlights

The Shadows/Highlights adjustment isn't a filter, but it acts like a Smart Filter in that can now be applied nondestructively. So choose Image > Adjustments > Shadow/Highlight.

By default, the Shadows/Highlights dialog box displays only a few sliders, but it offers much more control than that. Select the Show More Options box to see the full range.

3. Adjust the Sliders

First, move the Amount slider to 100% in both the Shadows and Highlights areas to pull out all possible detail. Then increase Midtone Contrast to 100% in the Adjustments area.

Next, adjust the Tonal Width sliders in the Shadows and Highlights areas. The Tonal Width sliders determine how exaggerated the effect will be.

Decreasing the Radius settings for either Highlights or Shadows or both will exaggerate the illustrated look by making the edges more obvious.

The Color Correction slider determines the saturation for the adjusted areas. Increase it to pop the colors, or decrease it to desaturate the image and make it look like an older illustration or an etching. Click OK to close the dialog box.

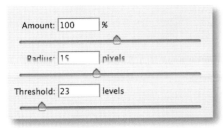

4. Apply the Unsharp Mask Filter

Next choose Filter > Sharpen > Unsharp Mask. For the illustrative effect, increase the Radius to exaggerate the edges, perhaps up to 15 pixels. The Amount determines how much sharpening takes place. Increase the Threshold to affect only the edges and not subtleties like the gray tones. Click OK.

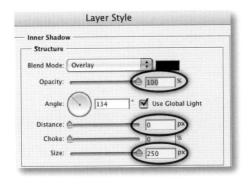

5. Add a Vignette Using a Layer Style

Use the Inner Shadow effect to apply a vignette: Click the Add A Layer Style icon at the bottom of the Layers palette and choose Inner Shadow. Move the Distance to 0 so the shadow will extend equally in all directions. Then, increase the Size of the shadow. Add as much or as little as you like. Set the Noise slider to 1%.

You can change the opacity and blending mode for the Inner Shadow to change the intensity of the vignette.

Super Smart Image Popping

Pull your subject out of the background with an enhanced Clarity effect using the High Pass filter.

TIP

Converting Multiple Layers. You can Shift-click a range of layers to select them, and then right-click and choose Convert To Smart Object. Then you can apply the filter to a combination of all of those layers at once.

1. Open the Image as a Smart Object

Smart Objects give you tremendous flexibility because you can apply filters without affecting the original pixels in the image. Also, any effect you create with Smart Filters can easily be shared with other files by dragging and dropping the stack of filters from a Smart Object in one document to a Smart Object in another. You can open your image as a Smart Object through Camera Raw, or convert it to a Smart Object in Photoshop by right-clicking on the layer name and choosing Convert To Smart Object.

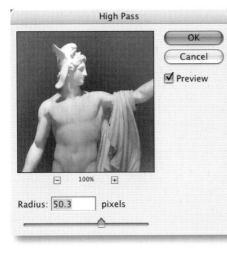

2. Apply the High Pass filter

Choose Filter > Other > High Pass. The High Pass filter exaggerates the contrasting edge details, and it ignores the rest of the image so that the subject really stands out. However, when you first apply the High Pass filter with its low default setting, the entire image becomes 50% gray (this isn't your goal, of course). It will take the magic of a Blend Mode in step 3 to fully create the subject-popping effect.

At a lower setting, the High Pass filter is similar to the Clarity slider in ACR, but at a higher Radius it can do much more. For this image, assigning a radius of 50 pixels will give a subtle transition between the darkening of the edge around the subject and the lightening of the subject itself. Click OK.

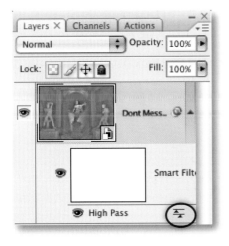

3. Choose a Blend Mode

Next, blend the High Pass filter effect with the original image. Double-click the icon to the right of the High Pass filter in the Layers palette. Then change the Blend Mode to Overlay or Soft Light; both are Contrast blending modes that neutralize the midtone grays introduced by the filter. Click OK.

The subject matter now appears to have been pulled out of the background. In fact, the center-most statue in this image looks as if you'd hand-painted an elaborate dodge and burn all the way around it.

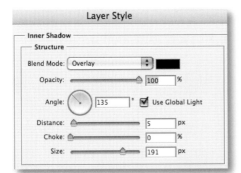

4. Add a Vignette

Click the Add A Layer Style icon in the Layers palette and choose Inner Shadow. Set the Distance to 0 and increase the Size to create a large vignette. Apply the blending mode you used for the filter (Soft Light or Overlay) so the darkening along the edge is also a dodge-and-burn effect.

Adding Density and Diffused Glows

Use this technique to add density to colors in an image, or to add a glow as well—whether mild or intense.

The technique is the same for each of these effects; the primary difference is the blending mode you apply, and the fine-tuning of what's visible using our secret Blend If sliders.

MODEL: CORRENE ©JHDAVIS

T I P

Merging Multiple Layers into One Duplicate. Duplicating a single layer is easy, but if you want to create this technique based upon several visible layers (for example, a set of layers that include retouching of Adjustment Layers), you'll want a shortcut for copying all the layers into one. Press Ctrl-Alt-E (Windows) or Command-Option-E (Mac OS) to make a single merged duplicate of all the currently visible layers in the document.

Basic Technique

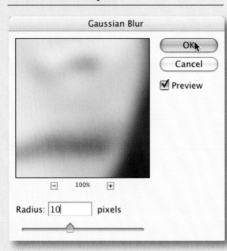

First, duplicate the current layer and put the copy on its own layer (see the tip at the left). Now change the new layer's Blend Mode to Soft Light (we'll try another mode later).

Next, choose Filter > Blur > Gaussian Blur to soften the image. How much blur you use depends on whether you want to exaggerate a glow or hide subtleties within the image.

To retain highlight and shadow detail that can sometimes be lost with these techniques, click the Add A Layer Style icon in the Layers palette, and choose Blending Options. Move the black triangle in the **This Layer** slider in the **Blend If** area to reveal detail in the shadows. Press Option/Alt as you click the triangle to split it. Use the halves to create a smooth transition between what's been hidden and what's completely visible. Use the white triangle the same way to bring back highlight detail if necessary.

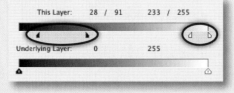

Adding a Subtle Effect

MODEL: CORRENE ©JHDAVIS

The **Soft Light** Blend Mode was used here for a subtle effect. Soft Light is one of the contrast, or dodge-and-burn, blending modes, so it lightens the lights and darkens the darks. It can be a nice way to add density to an image. Used here, the Soft Light blending mode softens detail throughout the image, intensifies the colors, and adds overall oomph.

In a portrait such as this one, the Soft Light blending mode adds richness in the hair, intensifies the background and the lips, and softens the skin.

Creating Intensity with Overlay

Exaggerating a Glow with Screen

Adding Density with Multiply

By switching our blurred duplicate layer to the Overlay Blend Mode (another Contrast Blend Mode), we create a more intense version of the effect. We also increase color saturation, as well as contrast. If you like the contrast and softness but not the saturation, you can choose Image > Adjustments > Hue/Saturation to fine-tune the intensity.

For a high-key exaggerated effect, use the Screen blending mode. It subtracts everything on the duplicate layer from the original, creating a true glowing high-key look.

When you use the Screen blend mode, adjust the Blend If sliders so that you see just the portion of the image where you want to keep the glow. For example, in a portrait, you may want to keep a little extra light around the cheek, chin, and nose, but not the entire image.

For a more exaggerated glow, move the black triangles in Blend If sliders to the right so that more of the original image is showing.

The Multiply blending mode is the opposite of the Screen blending mode. The Multiply blending mode is a great way to add substantial density to an image.

In this image, the reds in the skin are particularly enhanced. Again, use the Blend If slider to target exactly where you want the increased density visible. 🔳

Blend If: Gray

| This Layer: | 111 / 231 | 240 / 255 |

Underlying Layer: 0   255

Neutral and Gradient Overlay "Filters"

Replace a traditional graduated neutral density filter with a gradient and blending mode in Photoshop.

INSIGHT

Color! You can use this same effect with a custom color gradient. For example, use a dark-blue-to-yellow gradient to darken clouds and exaggerate a sunset.

New Layer

Name: Gradient Fill 1   OK

☐ Use Previous Layer to Create Clipping Mask   Cancel

Color: ☐ None

Mode: Overlay   Opacity: 100 ▸ %

---

1. Add a Gradient Fill Layer

A graduated neutral density filter is a piece of glass—darker at the top and clear at the bottom—that you put in front of your camera lens to get a more consistent exposure, allowing you to darken the sky without darkening what's below. If you don't have a graduated neutral density filter, you can achieve a similar effect in Photoshop.

First, set the foreground and background colors in the Tools palette to the default colors of black in the foreground and white in the background. Pressing D restores the default colors quickly.

Then, press Option/Alt as you click the Create New Adjustment Layer icon in the Layers palette, and choose Gradient. Name the layer and apply the Overlay blending mode. Click OK to create the gradient fill layer.

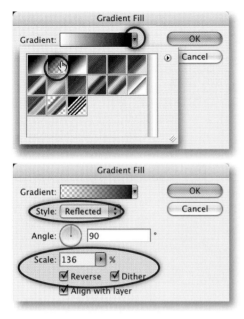

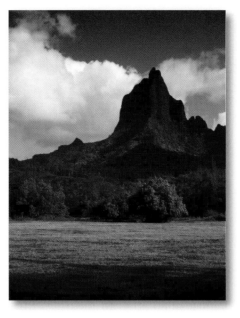

2. Customize the Gradient

In the Gradient Fill dialog box, select a gradient. To imitate a graduated neutral density filter, select the second gradient in the option box, the one that goes from Foreground to Transparent. Choose Linear for the style if you want the gradient to simply go from dark to neutral; or choose Reflected to go from dark to neutral to dark again, as when you want to darken both the sky and the lower portion of the image. Click and drag within your image to move the gradient up or down. To create a more gradual transition from dark to light, increase the Scale.

Because you've chosen the Overlay Blend Mode, where the gradient layer is black, the image is darkened. Where it's 50% gray, it has no effect on the image.

Click OK to accept the gradient.

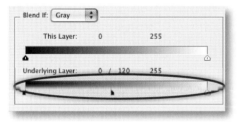

3. Adjust the Blend If Sliders

You can fine-tune the darkening taking place in your image by using the Blend If sliders. Select the gradient layer, click the Add A Layer Style icon in the Layers palette, and choose Blending Options. In the Blend If area of the dialog box, move the black stop in the Underlying Layer slider to give priority to the shadow detail in the layer beneath the gradient layer. Then, press Option/Alt and click the slider to split it. Separate the slider halves to create a smooth transition. The dark top of the peak now shows more shadow detail, even though the dark part of the gradient is on top of it.

INSIGHT

Underlying Layer. The current layer (This Layer) has the gradient. So you need to manipulate the Underlying Layer sliders to give priority to your background instead.

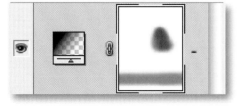

4. Paint in Detail

To further control where to show or hide the effect of the gradient, use the layer mask that came with the gradient fill layer. Select it, and paint with black anywhere that you want to pull out more detail. Lower the opacity of the brush for more flexibility. ▥

Creating Artistic Noise Overlay

Add Film Grain noise to cover banding in an image or to give your image a bit of an aged look.

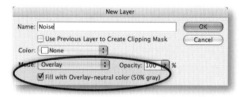

1. Add a Noise Layer

Press Option/Alt and click the Create A New Layer icon at the bottom of the Layers palette. Name the layer Noise. Change its blending mode to Soft Light (subtle) or Overlay (more contrast). Then select Fill With Neutral color (50% gray). Adding a fill content to the layer lets you apply a filter to it. Click OK.

2. Apply the Add Noise Filter

Zoom in to 100% to see detail. Then, choose Filter > Noise > Add Noise. Select Gaussian to distribute the noise more like the grain in traditional film. Also, film grain has no color artifacts, so select Mono-chromatic if you want that look. Set the Amount: 1 or 2 to hide inherent banding, 10 or higher to create more pronounced "artistic" noise. Click OK.

T I P

Change the Intensity. Because the noise is on its own layer, you can tone it down by lowering the layer's opacity.

3. Apply the Despeckle Filter

Now choose Filter > Noise > Despeckle. The Despeckle filter clumps the noise together more like film grain. Choose Filter > Blur > Blur Filter if you'd like to soften the effect. ▥

Adding a Custom Texture Overlay

Create a stain texture or a grunge look by overlaying one photograph on top of another.

©JHDAVIS

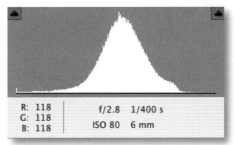

R: 118	f/2.8 1/400 s
G: 118	
B: 118	ISO 80 6 mm

1. Prepare the Image

An overlaid image can add texture without affecting color or tone. To prepare the texture image, open it in Camera Raw. Click Auto to set the black and white points. Then, select the HSL/Grayscale tab, and select Convert To Grayscale.

Adjust the Brightness slider until the hump in the histogram is centered, so that most of the tone in the image is roughly 50% gray. For more dramatic texture, increase the Contrast.

2. Add the Image to the Document

Click Open Object. In Photoshop, drag the image thumbnail from the Layers palette onto the target document. Change the blending mode to Overlay or Soft Light to make the medium grays transparent but leave the lighter and darker textures in the layer.

3. Position the Overlay Image

If you need to scale the texture, choose Edit > Free Transform, and then use the Free Transform tools to Scale, Flip, Warp, or otherwise transform the texture. When it's in position, double-click to set the transformation.

Shifting Your Focus

Imitate a shallow depth-of-field by blurring background elements to draw attention to the main subject of your image.

©JHDAVIS

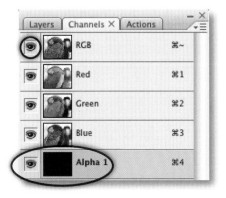

1. Duplicate the Layer

This technique depends on the Lens Blur filter, which requires a traditional "non-smart" layer. To protect the original photograph, duplicate the layer.

To create a single, flattened layer from a Smart Object or multiple visible layers, press Command-Option-Shift (Mac OS) or Ctrl-Alt-Shift (Windows) while you type N and then E on the keyboard. The N key creates a new layer and the E key turns it into a merged copy.

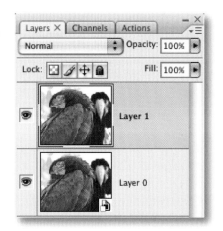

2. Create an Alpha Channel

A depth map lets you target the effects of the Lens Blur filter. The easiest way to create a depth map is to use an alpha channel. To create one, click the Create New Channel icon at the bottom of the Channels palette. (If the Channels palette isn't open, choose Window > Channels.)

The new channel is automatically an alpha channel, and it appears black. To see the image through the channel, make the RGB channels visible.

3. Paint a Depth Map

Paint the areas that you want to keep sharp. Start with a fully opaque, mid-sized paintbrush. Paint the edges of the subject matter you want to have in focus.

To see what you've painted, hide the RGB channels. With only the alpha channel showing, it's easier to fill in the rest of the subject area. You may want to reduce the opacity of the brush to paint just outside the subject area, so the background will blur more gradually.

Before you leave the Channels palette, make the RGB channels active by clicking on the RGB name, and hide the alpha channel.

4. Apply the Lens Blur Filter

Choose Filter > Blur > Lens Blur. In the Lens Blur dialog box, choose Alpha 1 from the Source menu in the Depth Map area. The Lens Blur filter uses the depth map to determine which areas of the image to blur. Increase the Radius, which controls how much blur is applied.

By default, the area you painted is blurry and the rest of the image is clear. Select Invert. Now the subject in the foreground is sharp, and the background is out of focus.

5. Add Noise

Adding a little noise can help the newly blurred areas match the inherent noise of the original. To make the foreground match the background, add some noise using the option in the Lens Blur dialog box: In the Noise area of the dialog box, move the Amount slider over just a bit; a setting of 1 or 2 is probably plenty. Then select Gaussian for a more natural-looking random noise distribution. Click OK. 🔲

CHAPTER 14
Black & White, Tinting, and Hand-Coloring Techniques

REMOVING THE COLOR of the natural world from our photographs immediately transports us into the wonderful realm of "interpreting" reality. By taking advantage of ACR's and Photoshop's remarkable range of options to shape the light and shadow, tone and texture, and "ying and yang" of our images, we can sculpt scenes of surreal monochromatic simplicity that just isn't possible with traditional color. But if you want the best of both creative worlds (color and non-color), that's possible, too, by tinting or bringing back the color in an antiqued fashion, thus having your proverbial cake and eating it, too.

Black-and-White Techniques in Photoshop

There are many ways to convert color images to black-and-white from within Photoshop, and to enhance those images as well.

Converting Images to Black-and-White in Photoshop

Photoshop CS3 introduced the **Black & White adjustment layer** to make it easier to convert images to black-and-white or grayscale. As with other Adjustment Layers, Black & White adjustment layers are nondestructive. One great advantage to using them is that you can lighten or darken specific color areas by dragging your cursor over the image itself. You can even apply multiple Black & White adjustment layers and use layer masks to apply the best portion of each of them.

The **Channel Mixer** is another great way to convert images to black-and-white, and potentially it can do so with fewer artifacts than a Black & White adjustment layer.

Infrared Effects

It's a little more challenging to achieve an infrared effect in Photoshop than it is in Camera Raw (which we'll cover on page 185), but you can do it. There is even an infrared preset in the Black And White dialog box, though it will not give you a true infrared look.

To apply an infrared look to an image (typically a scene with light foliage and a dark sky), click the Create New Adjustment Layer icon at the bottom of the Layers palette, and choose Black & White. Then, in the Black and White dialog box, move the Greens and Yellows sliders to the right until you start to lose detail, and then back down. The trick is to adjust the colors as far as you can without losing detail. Be sure to zoom in to see how the image is changing—especially to check for the introduction of unwanted noise.

Using Multiple Adjustment Layers

©JHDAVIS

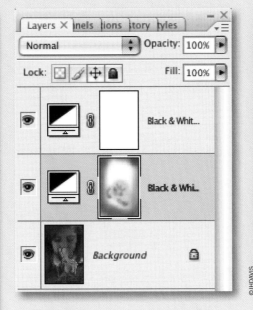

You can apply multiple Black & White adjustment layers, each one customized for a different look, and then use layer masks to pull portions all together.

First, click the Create New Adjustment Layer icon at the bottom of the Layers palette, and choose Black & White. In the Black And White dialog box, select a preset or adjust the colors you want to use. For portraits, I like to start with the Red Filter preset because it softens skin and minimizes blemishes.

Drag the cursor within the image to darken or lighten specific areas. "Scrub" left to darken, right to lighten. Or move the sliders if you know which colors you want to tweak. Zoom in so that you can see whether you're introducing artifacts or noise, particularly when you're adjusting colors that are close to each other in the spectrum, such as magentas and reds. Because you'll create another Adjustment

Layer, it's okay to lose a little detail or to otherwise sacrifice some parts of the image for areas you want to enhance. Click OK, and then hide the Adjustment Layer you just made.

Next, add another Black & White adjustment layer. **Click Auto to create a generic black-and-white version of the file, retaining all the detail.** Depending on the changes you made in the first Adjustment Layer, you may want to further adjust the colors. But if you're just hoping to regain some detail, Auto should do the trick. Click OK.

Show both Adjustment Layers. The first one takes precedence, because it's lower in the stack. Use a layer mask to hide parts of the first layer and thus reveal detail from the second layer: Select the layer mask for the first layer. Then use a big, soft, and low-opacity brush to paint with black in areas where you want to recapture the detail. The mask reveals how the image was converted using the second Adjustment Layer.

Using the Channel Mixer

©JHDAVIS

The Channel Mixer is a tried-and-true tool for black-and-white conversions. It's a great way to convert images with less chance of introducing artifacts and noise.

First, click the Create New Adjustment Layer icon in the Layers palette, and choose Channel Mixer. Select Monochrome at the bottom of the Channel Mixer dialog box to neutralize the color of the image. Because the Channel Mixer provides access to only the red, green, and blue channels, which are about as far apart from each other as they can get on the color wheel, you can darken and lighten colors with less potential for banding or posterizing.

No matter which method you use, always keep an eye on the Histogram to see whether you're losing tonal detail. ▦

Working with Black-and-White in Camera Raw

Though Photoshop has features to convert images to black and white, Adobe Camera Raw gives you more flexibility and more control over the process. And its Split Toning capabilities are far superior to any of Photoshop's Tinting capabilities.

Using Raw Files for Black and White Conversion

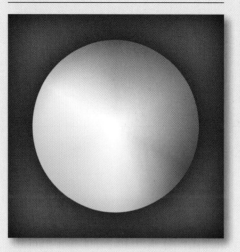

Higher bit-depth raw files are optimal when you're converting color images to grayscale. Instead of being limited to 256 shades per red, green, and blue primary colors (for a total of 16.7 million potential colors), they typically can use over 4,000 shades of red, green, and blue, for combined potential total of more than 60 billion colors. All those additional shades provide a superior black-and-white conversion.

TIP

Maintain Detail. Remember, maintaining detail throughout the tonal range of an image is central to quality. To make sure you don't clip any necessary shadow or highlight information in a photo, always have your Histogram palette open, and check it often!

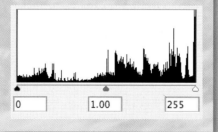

| 0 | 1.00 | 255 |

Dividing the Color Spectrum

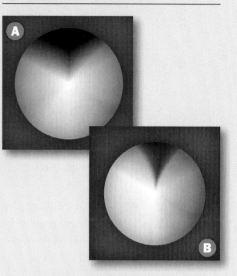

Camera Raw divides up the color spectrum differently from the Black & White adjustment layer in Photoshop. There's a big difference, for example, between the area that Photoshop categorizes as Reds **A** and the area that Camera Raw recognizes as Reds **B**.

Camera Raw also includes a separate (and indispensable) Oranges slider, so you have more control over skin tone. It also includes a Purples spectrum that isn't available in Photoshop. ▥

© JHDAVIS

Creating an Infrared Look

Though far from being a true representation of infrared's invisible spectrum, the ability to create dramatic black-and-white landscapes is easy with ACR's grayscale tools.

1. Convert the Image to Grayscale

The infrared look of light foliage and dark skies is particularly compelling in landscape images. But no matter what type of image you use, begin by converting it to grayscale. On the HSL/Grayscale panel, select Convert To Grayscale. Now the Grayscale Mix tab is the only one active. I typically start with all the settings at 0. I appreciate the Auto offer to take a stab at the conversion, but I'll determine the story I want to tell, thank you very much!

2. Adjust the Colors

Move the Greens and Yellow sliders to the right to lighten trees and grass. Infrared photographs typically have dark skies, so drop the Blue down to taste. The Aquas may need to be lightened or darkened, depending on the colors in the image.

Keep your eye on the histogram to make sure you're not losing any tonal detail. Also zoom in on the image to make sure you are maintaining texture detail in the light areas and not introducing noise into the dark areas. 🔲

©JHDAVIS

Antique "Hand-Tinting" of Photographs

Transform a modern image into an old-fashioned hand-tinted postcard, without needing dyes, pants, or a smock.

HTW **See page 27** to learn how to locate this book's follow-along images, cinematic tutorials, downloadable freebies, and useful links!

1. Ensure the Image is in RGB Color Mode

In the old days, all photos were black-and-white, and professional tinters painted color onto the surface of the photograph. To create a hand-painted look in Photoshop, you typically start with a black-and-white image. But because you're adding color, make sure you're in a color mode, not grayscale.

Choose Image > Mode, and then choose RGB Color.

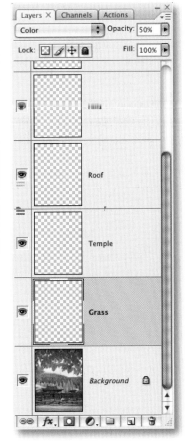

2. Choose your Color Palette

Hand-tinters worked quickly, somewhat sloppily, and with a very limited palette of dyes or pigments. To imitate their work, identify the key areas in your image, such as grass, rooftops, hair, or ocean. Then, choose a color to paint each key area.

Create the swatches you want to use. To add a swatch, change the foreground color in the Tools palette, and then click in an empty space in the Swatches palette to add that color. It might be handy to name the swatch for the area you want to paint with it, such as Sky. You can add as many swatches as you want, but to imitate a traditional hand-tinted look, limit the number of swatches for the image to just a handful.

3. Add a Layer for Each Element

The easiest way to tint the image (with the most control fine-tuning later) is to work with each color on a different layer. Press Option/Alt as you click the Create A New Layer icon in the Layers palette. Name each layer for its element, such as Grass, Roof, or Sky. While you're in the New Layer dialog box, set the Opacity to 50% and the blending mode to Color. The Color blending mode applies only the color from the layer, so the luminosity of the original image won't be affected. Setting the layer's Opacity to 50% lets you increase or decrease its Opacity after you've added paint, so that you can easily change a color's intensity without needing to paint more.

INSIGHT

One Layer or Many? You could paint the entire image on one layer, but painting on separate layers gives you greater flexibility. For example, you can adjust the opacity or change the blending mode for a single layer without affecting the other colors.

4. Paint!

Remember that the painters in the studio worked quickly and were a bit sloppy. A big soft brush gives you that effect. To paint a large area, you might start off with a brush size of 125, with Hardness set to 0. Also, set the Opacity to 50% to start. You can adjust the brush size and opacity as you work.

Select the first layer, then click the color swatch that corresponds to it. Now paint!

Paint each element, selecting its layer and then the swatch. Paint quickly. Feel free to "paint outside the lines." No one will mistake this for a real color photograph, so you can relax and play around with the look. Change the brush size and Opacity as you work on different elements. Remember that the square bracket keys change the brush size, and the numeric keys change the brush opacity.

5. Adjust the Opacity

After you've painted all the layers, some may be a little more or less intense than you like. Fine-tune the intensity of each color simply by changing the Opacity of its layer. Tweak the Opacity of each layer to find the balance that works.

6. Apply Blending Modes

The *Color* blending mode brings in only the color from the layer. But if you've applied color to an area that's white or very light in the original photo, the color may not show up, even at a high layer Opacity. You may find that for some layers, you want to use an additive mode, such as Multiply, to darken the effect. This is the equivalent of changing from translucent dyes to opaque pigments.

If you do use a blending mode to force color into an area such as the sky, you will probably want to adjust the layer's Opacity again.

TIP

Global Opacity. To change the Opacity of multiple layers at once, Shift-select them in the Layers palette and then drag them to the Create A New Group folder icon at the bottom of the Layers palette. Then set the Opacity of this entire group to taste.

You don't take a photograph, you make it.

—ANSEL ADAMS

IV

PREPARING TO PRINT

©SKYDHI9

CHAPTER 15
Getting Ready for Output

IN THE CASE OF PHOTOSHOP and printing, *dios* is in the details, specifically in global and targeted sharpening, removing noise and edge artifacts, and ultimately proofing and printing our masterpieces, either to our own desktop wonders, or by sending them out to a photo printing specialist.

©JHDAVIS

Global Sharpening

Enhance the details, not the distractions. Take advantage of the sharpening features in Camera Raw.

HTW **See page 27** to learn how to locate this book's follow-along images, cinematic tutorials, downloadable freebies, and useful links!

1. Adjust the Amount Slider

Camera Raw provides the best possible global sharpening, better even than you can achieve in Photoshop. When you need to sharpen an image, open it in Camera Raw, and then open the Detail panel. Zoom in to 100% or greater, so you can preview the changes. To zoom to 100% immediately, double-click the Zoom tool magnifying glass icon.

Start by increasing the Amount dramatically. The Amount determines the intensity of the sharpening, and exaggerating the sharpening shows you where artifacts might develop and what the following sliders are doing. You'll adjust the other sliders, and then return to fine-tune the Amount slider later. In this image, you want to sharpen the details **A** without exaggerating distracting background detail, such as the noise in the blurred background **B**.

2. Set a Low Radius

The Radius sets the pixel area that Camera Raw analyzes as it sharpens. Keep the Radius as low as possible to minimize artifacts. You can even set it below one pixel, down to .8 or .9, to perform subpixel sharpening. Press Option/Alt as you drag the Radius slider to see the area Camera Raw analyzes as it sharpens.

Typically, the only time you'll want to use a Radius larger than a pixel is to compensate for an image that's slightly out of focus.

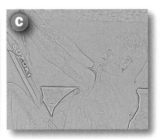

3. Keep the Detail Low

Keep the Detail setting as low as possible to prevent artifacts. Even with the slider at 0, you'll see some sharpening **A**. At 100, every edge and texture artifact is sharpened **B**. For landscapes you can use more, for portraits, less. For this photo the slider was set at 25. Press Option/Alt as you move the slider to see the intensity change **C**.

4. Control Sharpening with Masking

The Masking slider is what makes ACR's Sharpening so effective. Masking reduces the appearance of artifacts in areas without contrast (such as skies or skin tones). As you increase the masking, sharpening occurs only along the more obvious edges. Press Option/Alt as you move the slider to see exactly what's being sharpened.

5. Make Final Adjustments

Now that you know how it all works, return to the Amount slider and lower it a bit. Because the Masking slider is so helpful, you can leave the Amount setting higher than you would otherwise, resulting in a significant increase in sharpness overall without sharpening the noise. ▦

Targeted Sharpening

To sharpen only a portion of an image, use the Smart Sharpen filter in Photoshop.

T I P

Open As Smart Object. Press Shift to switch the button in Camera Raw from Open Image to Open Object, or vice versa.

T I P

Sharpening a Merged Visible Copy. The only time you may not be able to take advantage of Smart Filters for sharpening is when you are attempting it in a file with multiple layers at the end of your workflow. In that case it may be easier to make a Merged Visible copy of all the layers in the file by pressing Command-Option-Shift-NE (Mac OS) or Ctrl-Alt-Shift-NE Windows) and sharpening and masking that layer.

Layers × |els |ory |rles |ons |ths	
Normal	Opacity: 100%
Lock:	Fill: 100%
03-Bee

1. Open as a Smart Object

Smart Objects give you access to nondestructive Smart Filters, and that's exactly what you'll want to use to sharpen a targeted portion of your image.

So, if you've used Camera Raw to perform global edits, click Open Object to open it in Photoshop as a Smart Object. If you haven't used Camera Raw for your image, choose File > Open As Smart Object, and then select the image. The icon in the corner of the layer thumbnail indicates that it's a Smart Object.

2. Apply the Smart Sharpen Filter

Choose Filter > Sharpen > Smart Sharpen. In the Smart Sharpen dialog box, increase the Amount to a ridiculously high value. Set the Radius below a pixel unless you're trying to compensate for an image that's out of focus.

Choose Lens Blur from the Remove menu. The default, Gaussian Blur, uses the same algorithm as the Unsharp Mask filter, but without the benefit of the Threshold slider. Lens Blur is a much more sophisticated algorithm.

Lower the Amount value, but keep it as high as you can get away with without getting artifacts. It's okay if there's sharpening in the background because you'll mask that out in the next step. For this sample image, you can set the Amount all the way up to 500%.

Click OK to apply the filter.

INSIGHT

When Less Is More. Typically the More Accurate option makes images look more like a mosaic—rarely more accurate! Deselect it.

Likewise, the Advanced options are usually more cumbersome than useful if you're trying to remove sharpening based on subject matter. Stick with the Basic options and a mask.

TIP

Before and After. In any filter window in Photoshop, click the Preview image within the dialog box to see the image before changes.

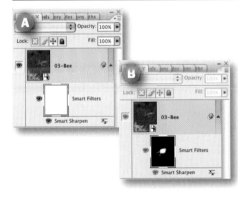

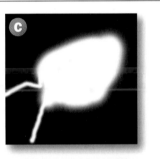

3. Limit Sharpening to the Subject

Smart Filters include a filter mask, which you'll use to mask out the areas you don't want sharpened. By default, the mask is white **A**, so the entire image is sharpened. You can paint with black to obscure areas you don't want to sharpen, but if you want to sharpen only a small area, fill the mask with black and then paint the areas with white to sharpen: Press D to reset the foreground and background colors to black and white. Clicking on the mask swaps foreground and background colors. Press Command/Ctrl-Delete to fill it with black. Then paint with white over the areas you want to sharpen **B**.

Paint with a soft brush and high Opacity.

To see the mask **C**, press Option/Alt as you click its thumbnail. You can paint directly on the mask to clean it up as needed. 🔲

INSIGHT

Why Not Use Unsharp Mask? The Unsharp Mask filter has a nifty Threshold slider, which works somewhat like the Masking slider in Camera Raw. However, the filter mask that comes along with Smart Filters is more useful for targeted sharpening because it lets you limit which areas in the image are affected, to support the story you want to tell.

Removing Noise and Fringe Artifacts

Pixel texture made up of random color or luminosity called *noise* distracts from the story you want to convey. General noise and artifacts that fringe edges in an image typically result from oversharpening, the way the light bends through the lens at the time the image is shot, or overediting that exposes detail in an image. Reducing noise and fringing can be tricky, but both can be minimized with the Noise Reduction feature in ACR.

Using Noise Reduction Sliders

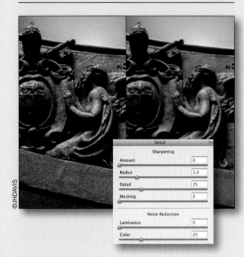

There are two main types of noise: **luminance** (also called **contrast**) and **chroma** (also called **color**). The Noise Reduction sliders on the Detail tab in Camera Raw attempt to remove both kinds of noise.

Color noise is pretty easy to remove—essentially, the slider blurs the color noise and blends it back in. Move the Color slider to the right to remove color noise. A setting of about 5 is a good place to start, but the optimal value depends on both the noise and the other color characteristics of the image.

Luminance noise is trickier. You can try to remove luminance noise using the Luminance slider in Camera Raw, but it often clumps the noise instead of removing it. That's because Camera Raw can't differentiate between detail you want to keep and the noise you want to remove. You may want to try the Luminance slider, and if it works for your image, great. Otherwise, you'll probably have better luck using some of the powerful specialized third-party software like Noiseware Pro, discussed on the facing page.

Correcting Chromatic Aberration

The Lens Corrections panel in ACR contains the Chromatic Aberration controls. **Chromatic aberration** is caused by the way the spectrum of light is bent through the lens when the image is taken, and it occurs frequently with low-quality or extremely wide-angle lenses. To correct chromatic aberration, the sliders let you rebend the different color channels—red, green, and blue—distorting and scaling them independently to bring them back into better alignment.

There are two sliders. Start with the one that adjusts the colors most prominently fringing in your image. For example, in this image, yellow and blue aberrations are most apparent, so you'd start with the Fix Blue/Yellow Fringe slider. Then, adjust the other slider to try to balance the colors effectively.

Choose an option from the Defringe menu, introduced with Camera Raw 4.1, to defringe highlight edges where the problem is often most apparent, or all edges in the image.

As a bonus, correcting color aberrations and defringing an image can also help remove much of the luminance and color noise.

Using Third-Party Filters

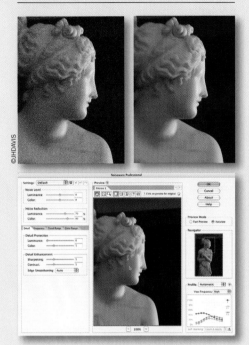

©JHDAVIS

If you frequently need to remove noise from images, consider investing in one of the excellent third-party filters that work with Photoshop.

Noiseware Pro from Imagenomic works with Smart Objects as a Smart Filter, so it can remove the noise in an image non-destructively. And it's amazing, really. The filter has presets for landscape, portrait, film grain effect, and other situations, but often the Default setting does an excellent job! I use Noiseware Pro all the time, especially when I'm working with images I shot with a pocket camera.

Another one to look into is DFine from Nik Software. There are many fine companies creating filters and plug-ins that extend the capabilities of Photoshop, and if there's a task you perform frequently, such add-ons can be a smart investment.

Defringing with a Blending Mode

©JHDAVIS

Fringing is a common issue in images that have been oversharpened, a problem that isn't related to chromatic aberration or misalignment—and one that can't be fixed in Camera Raw. You'll need to defringe such an image in Photoshop.

The trick to removing this kind of fringing is to add a layer that can only darken or lighten, so you can remove a dark or light halo. Start by creating a new layer. Press Option/Alt as you click the Create New Layer icon in the Layers palette, so the New Layer dialog box opens. Name the layer, and then choose a blending mode. If you want to remove a light halo, choose Darken; if you're removing a dark fringe, choose Lighten. If you're trying to remove a color fringe, choose the Color blending mode. Click OK.

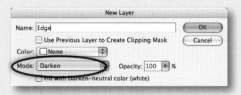

Now, use the Brush tool, with a small brush and Opacity set to around 75%. Press Option/Alt to change the tool to the eyedropper so you can sample a color. With the new empty layer active, sample an area you want to replace the fringe with. That is, sample a color that would be there if the fringe were gone. If you're trying to remove a light fringe, sample a color that is darker than the fringe but lighter than much of the image, so it won't affect the darker areas. Then, paint over the fringe. You may want to resample as you paint different areas.

With the Darken blending mode, the layer can only darken the file, not lighten it. The opposite is true for the Lighten blending mode (hence the name). Change the Opacity of the Brush to control how much you darken or lighten the fringed area.

©JHDAVIS

Soft-Proofing and Print Previewing

Accurately previewing your image on-screen lets you optimize it for a particular device before you print.

Mapping Gamuts. Every device has a gamut that defines the range of colors it can recognize and reproduce. The eye can see the broadest range of colors, followed by the gamuts for Wide Gamut **A**, Adobe RGB **B**, and sRGB **C**. Overlapping the RGB gamuts is the CMYK gamut **D**, which includes the colors that can be reproduced using cyan, magenta, yellow, and black in a traditional offset printing process. Unfortunately, there isn't as much overlap between the CMYK and RGB gamut as we would like, so color management systems, no matter how good they are, may not match colors perfectly.

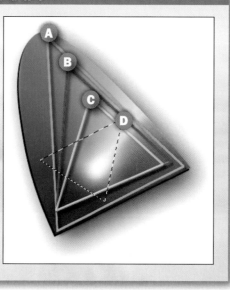

1. Obtain Appropriate Color Profiles

To accurately preview an image on-screen, or *soft-proof* it, you need to use the correct color profile for the device you plan to use for printing. For a desktop printer, profiles come with the printer. If you are sending the image to an outside source for printing, your service bureau should provide you with profiles. Install profiles at the operating system level so Photoshop and other applications can access them.

For the most accurate preview, use a profile that specifies not only the device, but also the ink set, paper stock, and printer resolution.

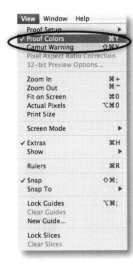

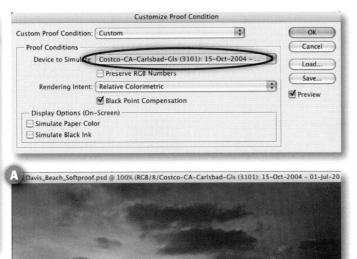

A

2. Soft-proof the Image

Choose View > Proof Setup > Custom. In the Customize Proof Condition dialog box, choose the profile from the Device To Simulate menu. Unless a service provider or your printer documentation tells you otherwise, select Relative Colorimetric for the rendering intent, and select Black Point Compensation. Click OK to set the custom profile.

If Proof Colors is checked in the View menu, the title bar for your image now includes the color space you're previewing, and the image appears as it would when printed on the device you specified **A**. Press Command/Ctrl-Y to toggle the Proof Colors command on and off.

3. Correct Any Problems

Because color spaces don't map perfectly, you may need to adjust the color in portions of your image for a specific device. For example, the highly saturated orange detail around the sun **A** went outside the gamut of a specific Costco profile. It changed to a bright lime green **B**, which leaves the image muddy and makes the print unusable.

Adjusting the Color. To edit a specific portion of the tonal range using a Hue/Saturation adjustment layer, select a color group from the Edit menu, and drag the adjustment sliders to a very tight portion of the spectrum. Then, shift the Hue and Saturation sliders all the way to the right. The top bar shows the color before you make changes and the bottom bar is the current color. With the eyedropper, click the colors to adjust in the image. The sliders move to represent the colors you selected. Everything between the bars is adjusted. Drag the triangle sliders farther apart to create a smoother transition. Next, make the actual adjustment: zero out the sliders and then either desaturate or shift the hue.

To bring the colors in your document into the reproducible gamut of your destination printer, make temporary changes while Proof Colors is selected. Adjust the color using any method you like, but be sure to do it nondestructively, as the changes are only appropriate for one particular device. The Hue/Saturation adjustment layer is usually a good choice, as it lets you target a very specific color range and doesn't make any changes to your original.

When you've made the changes, name the new layer for the device you're targeting so you'll remember to hide that layer if you print elsewhere, and you'll be able to find it if you print to the same device in the future.

4. Duplicate the Image

To ensure that your master remains unaffected—and that *no one can reset adjustment layers in the file* you send to your output provider—duplicate and flatten it: Choose Image > Duplicate. Select Duplicate Merged Layers Only, and click OK.

If the bottom layer was called *Background*, Photoshop automatically flattens the file. If the bottom layer had a different name, flatten the layers manually: Choose Flatten Image from the Layers palette menu.

Convert to Profile

Source Space
Profile: Adobe RGB (1998)

Destination Space
Profile: Costco–CA–Carlsbad–Gls (3101): 15–Oct–2004 – ...

Conversion Options
Engine: Adobe (ACE)
Intent: Relative Colorimetric
☑ Use Black Point Compensation
☑ Use Dither
☐ Flatten Image

5. Convert the Color Space

Though you've been previewing the image in the color space for the device profile, the image itself is still in its original color space. You need to convert it before you send it to a service provider. Choose Edit > Convert To Profile. In the Convert To Profile dialog box, choose the destination profile from the menu as you did in the View menu. Click OK.

Choose File > Save, and save the image in the format the service bureau recommended, such as JPEG or TIFF. Select Embed Color Profile, and select the maximum quality possible for the image file.

Now relax. Because you've soft-proofed the file, you shouldn't face any surprises. ▥

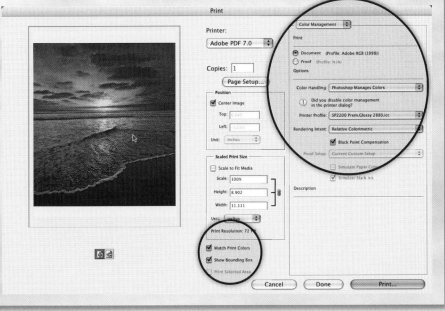

Index

A

B

C

H

hair
    blending changes around hairlines,
        106
    intensifying wisps of, 63
    patching, 108–109
halos in replaced backgrounds, 63
HDR (High Dynamic Range), 80
Heal mode (Retouch tool), 88
Healing Brush tool
    healing wrinkles, 110–111
    patching skin, 107
    removing shine with, 105–106
    Retouch tool vs., 159
    sampling all layers with, 105
    smoothing color banding, 147
hiding/showing all palettes, 14
High Pass filter, 171
highlights
    altering specular, 116
    bringing back lips', 131
    editing Smart Object to pull out, 77
    patching detail in, 148–150
    protecting areas of tonal range, 68–69
    reinserting pupils' specular, 129
histograms
    finding optimal exposure with, 23
    watching when adjusting tonality, 173
How to Wow presets, 43
HSL presets, 44
HSL/Grayscale panel (Camera Raw)
    converting images to, 39, 49, 89
    infrared looks from, 185
    positioning sliders in gradual curve,
        49
    retouching images from, 89
Hue/Saturation dialog box
    adjusting sliders in, 100–101
    exaggerating skin tone, 99
    using Hue/Saturation adjustment
        layers, 98

I

icons, 13
images. See also antique photo effects;
        portraits; previewing; retouching
        images
    adding metadata to, 30
    adjusting digital camera preferences
        for, 20–22
    archiving, 22
    assigning/converting color profiles
        for, 25
    batch processing, 33–34
    on CD-ROM copyrighted, 27
    changing contrast in, 121
    choosing camera's format for, 20
    colorizing or converting to grayscale,
        39
    combining for group portraits,
        140–141
    comparing, 31, 36
    converting to CMYK color space, 26
    copyright notices for, 30
    darkening edges of, 89
    deleting objects from, 139, 142–144
    dodging and burning, 72–75
    duplicating and protecting master,
        202
    editing in Camera Raw, 41–42
    finding optimal exposure, 23
    hand recoloring effects for, 162–163
    imitating shallow focus in, 178–179
    importing to Bridge, 30
    increasing clarity of, 42, 77
    infrared effects for, 182, 185
    intensifying fine lines of, 63
    labeling and rating, 31
    making multiple versions of one,
        76–77
    multiple tones in, 70–71
    noise reduction of, 39
    opening as Smart Objects, 15, 40, 49
    optimizing photo taking, 22
    out-of-focus, 107
    painting highlight detail in, 148–150
    reducing vibrance, 164
    removing dust spots on, 88, 95
    retouching, 37, 49, 151–153
    saving in Camera Raw, 40
    sharing duplicate of, 53
    sharpening, 21
    sorting and rejecting, 32
    stacking, 31
    synchronizing settings for all, 36
    tinting, 158–159, 160–161, 186–189
    transferring from camera to computer,
        22
    viewing clipping of, 38
importing images to Bridge, 30
infrared effects, 182, 185
Intelligent ISO feature, 21
intensifying fine lines, 63
ISO settings, 21

J

JPEG files, 15, 36

K

keyboard shortcuts
    adjusting brush opacity, 150
    brush size, 115
    changing Open Image to Open Object
        button, 196
    copying content to new layer, 134

W

JHDAVIS PHOTOGRAPHY
www.Adventures in Photoshop.com

JHDavis Photography
www.Adventures in Photoshop.com

JHDAVIS PHOTOGRAPHY
www.Adventures in Photoshop.com